# Bobs, Brush, and Brittanies

*A Long Love Affair with Quail Hunting*

## ALSO BY JOEL VANCE

*Grandma and the Buck Deer*
*Confessions of an Outdoor Maladroit*
*Billy Barnstorm, the Birch Lake Bomber*
*Bobs, Brush, and Brittanies*

# Bobs, Brush, and Brittanies

## A Long Love Affair with Quail Hunting

## Joel Vance

LYONS & BURFORD,
PUBLISHERS

Printed in the United States of America

10 9 8 7 6 5 4 3 2 1

Illustrations by Christopher J. Seubert
Design by Cindy LaBreacht

Library of Congress Cataloging-in-Publication Data
Vance, Joel M., 1934–
    Bobs, brush, and brittanies: a long love affair with quail hunting /
Joel Vance.
        p.    cm.
    ISBN 1-55821-588-3
    1. Quail shooting.   I. Title.
SK325.Q2V36     1997
799.2'4627—dc21                                        97-12162
                                                           CIP

MOST DEDICATIONS ARE SIMPLE:
*"To my beloved," which leaves the door open for the author to be cherished by any number of gullible people. By necessity, mine is a bit longer.*

———————

*First, this book (and my life) is dedicated to Marty— my strength, my eternally forgiving wife. Next, to my children: Carrie, J. B., Eddie, Andy, and Amy, who are more dear to me than the bird dogs. Honest.*

*Next, of course, to the bird dogs and especially to Guff, whose grave I still visit and who always will be a part of me.*

*Finally, to my hunting buddies, especially Dave Mackey, of the unerring eye; Spence Turner, who has been bumming around with me for a quarter century; and Foster Sadler, who did the same before he went on a longer and darker jaunt.*

*Then how should I begin*

*To spit out all the butt-ends of my days and ways?*

*And how should I presume?*

—

T. S. ELIOT, "THE LOVE SONG OF J. ALFRED PRUFROCK"

# CONTENTS

# ACKNOWLEDGMENTS

SOME OF THIS MATERIAL has appeared in slightly different form in various outdoor magazines, mostly *Gun Dog*, *Wing and Shot*, and *The Missouri Conservationist*. Thanks are due those publications and others for giving me space in the first place and for being kind enough to let me reuse the material here.

Thanks are also due the many people from whom I've swiped good stories, good recipes, and good experiences. I hope I've given credit where due, but if I forgot or didn't realize the roots of my material, please forgive me—it wasn't intentional.

# INTRODUCTION

SEVERAL YEARS AGO a friend and his quail-hunting partner started down a creek, one on each side, agreeing to meet at a crossing. When my friend didn't appear his partner went looking for him. He found him dead of a heart attack, his dog sitting close by.

Without exception, quail hunters would say, "Well, if I have to go, that's the way I want to do it."

Quail hunting is a love that cannot be denied. An old story sums it up: A lifelong quail hunter, finally brought to his deathbed, summons his weeping family.

"I know I've not been a good husband and father," he says weakly. "I've gone quail hunting on our anniversary and on your birthdays. I've let things slip around the house and never got ahead at work because I cared more about quail hunting than I did about my career. I've spent the family money on bird dogs and guns."

He pauses, then a faint smile creases his seamed face. "But," he says, "I sure shot a hell of a lot of birds."

As anyone within the range of quail knows, "bird" means "quail."

Quail. God, I love 'em. I grew up with quail. It was the bird of my childhood—more than that, it was about the only viable game animal in rural Missouri when I was old enough to carry a mule-kicking single-shot Stevens.

I've hunted pheasants, various grouses, doves, woodcock, and even waterfowl with my bird dogs, but their real job is hunting quail. So while I appreciate the value of George Bird Evans's Old Hemlock setters on a grouse hunt and I empathize with Burton Spiller as he follows his pointer's nose to a roosting woodcock, deep down I feel sorry for those guys—they could have been hunting *quail* with those dogs.

There is a masochistic streak in all quail hunters. We enjoy pain, or at least grin through it day after day, complaining only when the season ends and with it the nagging aches. It's analogous to the old joke about the Little Moron who enjoyed hitting himself on the head with a hammer because it felt so good when he stopped.

The difference is, quail hunters don't enjoy it when it stops. A quail hunter will gladly trudge fourteen miles, all uphill, plowing through briar thickets that scrape his hide into a city street map, all for something that weighs eight ounces on a good day.

Bobwhite quail are the most important of the upland birds in the thirty-seven states and two Canadian provinces where they are legal game. Only doves are more often taken (some 50 million, compared to 35 million bobwhites), but shooting doves is about as interesting as shooting starlings. Doves are just too stupid, even for birds.

Hunters take about 2.2 million valley quail, 1.3 million desert quail, and nearly 4 million blue quail—a long way from the bobwhite figures. The national kill of ruffed grouse, the bird deified by legendary outdoor writers, is less than 3 million. Combine the harvest of every gallinaceous game bird and it's still only about one-third the annual bobwhite quail bag.

So what is it about this little chicken that makes otherwise sound citizens act as if their brains were torn?

Perhaps it's because quail are available and they are gentlemanly in their habits. Give them food and cover and they thrive. They usually sit for a bird dog; they flush at unpredictable angles, presenting a shooting challenge; and they are exquisite on the table. No other bird has so many plusses with no minuses.

OUR OLD HUNTING shack near the Mussel Fork was a maple-shaded farmhouse perched on a hill in Adair County, bit by winds that filtered through the leafless maples and the million and one cracks of an old farmhouse.

It was still dark as I awoke in the unheated upstairs. The tip of my nose prickled where it peeked from the mountain of quilts. Gonna be a cold one.

My eyes were gritty from the day before and my face felt shaped by a wood rasp. Somebody's grandmother, sepia-toned by a century on the wall, glared down from an oval frame. The night before, I had quickly kicked off my clothing, racing with the icy cold. Now my neglected hunting garb got its revenge. It felt woven from hoarfrost.

Breakfast burbled on the stove downstairs, and the vibrant fragrance of coffee rolled up the stairwell. Those who had claimed the heated downstairs rose early; those of us huddled under quilts in the icy upstairs were reluctant to contact floors pale with frost.

Before we ventured into the whitened fields, we stoked our furnaces with the day's first dose of cholesterol, at the sight of which a cardiologist would instantly infarct. Animal fat is the quail hunter's constant companion. We start the day with half-cooked bacon and rich yellow eggs so shiny with grease they shoot down the gullet like ferrets down a rathole. Lunch will be fat-freckled salami, and supper probably some fried atrocity that triggers percussive indigestion and makes the hunting shack sound like an artillery duel.

At least that's the way it is if you hang around, as I do, with guys who cook the way senior citizens run hurdles. The exception is Spence Turner, who loves to eat well and has learned to cook so he can. Spence is chef by acclamation. Iron Man Spence is that rarity, a hunter who enjoys cooking.

Which reminds me of an old joke based on an even older camp rule: Anyone who complains about the food has to cook.

One afternoon, while the rest of the camp is out having fun, the hunter stuck with cook duty mopes through a pasture and spies a huge cow flop. *I know how to fix those guys,* he thinks. *I'll bake a cow-flop pie, and the first guy who complains has to do the cooking.* So he fixes this cow-flop pie, with a delicate, lattice-top crust, and serves it for supper.

A burly hunter shovels a huge bite of cow-flop pie into his mouth, sputters, "Good God Almighty! That's cow-flop pie!" Then he adds in a strained voice, "It's good, though."

OUT IN WHAT once was a smokehouse is a dog. Until two nights ago he had been your basic fireside pet, plump with the suet of inactivity and twitching amid dreams of former glory. Now he's been dumped into a prickly bed of cold straw with a couple of smelly strangers, shivering in the frosty night and listening to distant coons squall.

He'll come stiffly from the smokehouse, his amber eyes dark with the accusation that I have spent a warm, comfortable night inside. I could explain all I want about the icy bedroom, but he knows what he knows. He's also ready to forgive if I'll take him to the bird fields. His is a simple faith. He lives only to find birds. He is in the grip of genetic imperatives.

If you shoot well and quail rain from the sky, Dog is inordinately pleased and will find them and, if God has favored you, bring them to you in a mouth as tender as a baby's caress. (Or he may clamp them with hammer-mill jaws that squirt guts like toothpaste from a tube.)

If you miss, Dog doesn't turn and give you a slow burn, like

Jack Benny confronted with one of life's miseries, or snarl and roar, the way you do when he or she screws up. Dog just moves on and tries to find more game birds. The simple complexity of the bird dog.

BIRD DOGS HAVE pulled a thread through the smooth fabric of my life all the way back to Pat, a lovely, feathery-tailed English setter my father took as payment on a debt. Dad thought he had a good deal, but he was wrong, for Pat had a stone nose and a brain to match.

Years later, I bet that my bird dog was infinitely better than the dog of an outdoor-writer friend. We carried on a friendly feud in the public press, and people waited eagerly to see who would triumph when finally our dogs took the field together. Oh, how I flayed him in person and in print! His dog, I opined, was the inspiration for Jack Clement's tender ballad "That Dirty Old Egg-Sucking Hound." And so it went.

We finally hunted together—and my dog ate three of his quail. That was Chip, the first bird dog I really loved, even at that moment of extreme mortification.

It was Chip who greeted me that cold morning on the Mussel Fork. He was a Brittany, descended from the elders of the bird-dog tribe, for spaniels were pointing birds before the first pointer or setter ever hove onto the scene to eat his master's lunch or pee on the boss's hunting coat.

That was a long-off, sweetly remembered morning, for Chip is gone and one of the hunters from that hunting shack is gone and the shack has become a home for strangers, with carpets and a stove that works.

In memory, my breath hangs in the still morning air and I stretch luxuriously, hearing the faint popping of my abused skeletal structure. Off in the bottoms a quail whistles reveille. Time for all of us to get together—them hunched nervously in the fencerow, us trudging down the row on either side, stumbling over clods, stepping in chuckholes.

It's an ancient game we play, the stakes being somewhat higher for the quail.

We start into the quail jungles. The theory goes, when God created the world, He ran out of brains before He got to quail hunters, but He decided to go ahead anyway and throw in a pointer to boot. Then He realized this brainless pair needed habitat, so He created the bramble.

"Bramble" generically covers an array of plant life armed with weapons fierce enough to bring a Cape buffalo to its knees. Wild rose, blackberry, catbriar, plum, locusts—the names march on like the dread recitation of one's past sins on the Day of Judgment. And the punishment is just as severe as eternal damnation. I used to come home from a quail hunt looking as though I'd been waltzing with cougars, or at least I did until, at the age of fifty, I started wearing brush pants.

For a half century I had worn blue jeans or britches too shabby for the Salvation Army—and I wondered why my skin hurt at day's end. Brush pants or, even better, chaps are God's gift to dim bird hunters.

There was a time, so they tell me, when the bobwhite quail lurked at the edge of the fearsome thickets, only occasionally venturing into the spiky depths. Now the quail I meet over the bead of my old L. C. Smith are born in the briar patch. Hunting them is like being a field tester for barbed wire.

Our guns are burnished and silvered by miles of stiletto shrubbery, the finely figured stock wood scratched and gouged. When the covey goes up, the guns bark at them with the authority of their many years, and sometimes the quail listen.

Dogs and quail and old pards.

So what if there are days when the miles back to the car are far longer than those going in. So what if the best part of the day was a tired baloney sandwich. So what if sometimes I can't shoot my way out of a fertilizer sack with a case of field loads. So what if there are times when my dog couldn't point a roast beef sandwich in the middle of a snooker table. So what if we get up seven coveys and everyone limits out but me because I never once was in a position to shoot.

So what.

There's always tomorrow, when the dog I trained from spraddly puppyhood spawns a point so taut you couldn't move him with a D-7 Caterpillar, and the covey comes up and I take one neatly on the left then swing smoothly to the right and dump a second, and the dog retrieves them both without ruffling a feather and my old hunting pard scratches at his chinstubble and growls, "Damn, that was nice shooting."

# 1

# WHAT IS THIS THING CALLED BIRD?

CHARLIE ELLIOTT, who hunted more years than most people live, called quail the Prince of Game Birds. I guess that's because ruffed grouse are known as the King of Game Birds. Kings supposedly outrank princes, but kings often are doddering old windbags, while princes cut a wicked swath—look at the British Royal Family.

I'd rather chase a fiery young prince than a creaky monarch any day.

Bobwhite quail are the nation's number-one upland game bird. Only mourning doves are shot in greater numbers. But dove hunting isn't really hunting. You hunt only for a place to shoot. Skeet with feathers.

Grouse are flighty and unpredictable, prone to walk away from even the staunchest point. This must be frustrating for the dog, which did its job only to have the quarry ignore the rules. It's like a bowler throwing a strike only to have the pins pop back up.

Woodcock are wonderful for dogs, especially a skittery young one, but woodcock are solitary, not covey birds. It's a rare day when you find the legendary fall of woodcock, where points are common and shooting hot. You may get a flush of two birds and occasionally three, but you don't experience the incomparable explosion of a covey flush.

Pheasants won't hold and are mean and contrary to boot. Of all the game birds, partridge are the closest to quail, but chukars live in places that closely resemble Hell, and gray partridge aren't nearly as widespread as quail. Further, gray partridge tend to flush wild and fly far.

Only the bobwhite, bless his sweet heart, has it all together for the bird hunter. I have unashamedly loved quail hunting for more than forty years—actually closer to fifty, I guess.

I'm an average to often below-average shot, and my dogs are good but not great. I know quail habitat when I see it. I probably can find quail that most other hunters can't because I work harder than they do and I believe I have a feeling for where the birds might be. And I worked for a conservation agency for twenty-two years, mingling with professionals, and much of their knowledge rubbed off. Let's just say I have a jumble of quail lore stored away.

Even as I write this I'm reliving a hunt with a friend. When Kathy Love became editor of *The Missouri Conservationist*, she figured she'd better find out what all the hunting fuss is about. So she attended a Women in the Outdoors seminar in Arkansas, then traveled to Texas for a quail hunt. She couldn't hit the ground with her hat, but the excitement was building—the dogs pointed, birds flew, and the gun shouted. That's the nub of quail hunting anyway. Good shooting is a combination of innate skill and practice, and all quail hunters are eternally optimistic about their shooting. The next shot will be true and all shots after that.

I took Dacques and Chubby, my oldest and most reliable dogs, to impress Kathy with smooth dogwork. Chubby bumped the first bird, a woodcock. Then I made an incredible brush shot that no doubt had Kathy reeling with admiration (or maybe it was the tree she walked into in the confusion).

The dogs settled down and pointed a covey in the woods. Not believing birds would be roosting in the woods on a beautiful sunny day, I told the dogs to move on—and they flushed a nice covey. I fired a salute in the general direction of the Pleiades, then proceeded to miss three more good, if difficult shots, all over points. Kathy now believes that I have the world's greatest bird dogs—and don't deserve them.

Perhaps I've been responsible for creating another bird hunter. I doubt Kathy will force her husband to build a kennel for six bird dogs, our present total, or spend the vacation money on a new double. But she has felt the excitement of the chase, and once in the blood that fever will recur, like malaria.

It's a persistent and always low-grade fever; sometimes with me it's virulent. Chances are I won't hit most birds I find, but I'm often afield when the rest have quit. I'm the guy who gets restless on a Sunday afternoon drabbed by spitting sleet, calls the dog, and heads out for a miserable one-hour hunt before dark because the season is winding down and we never know how many seasons are left. If I didn't go it would bother me.

RESEARCHERS HAVE only recently begun to uncover the real secrets of quail, using tiny radio transmitters attached to the birds, like a bib. Quail don't always do what we've been taught to believe they do—like Kathy's covey holed up in the middle of a woodlot against all reason.

I spent a week walking "transects" (lines surveyed cross-country) at Missouri's Blind Pony Wildlife Area, the site of the Show-Me State's latest quail research. We started early in the morning, walked cross-country to near noon, then put in a couple to three hours in the afternoon—a long day's hunt.

Actually it was work, not hunting, for although I was using my bird dogs, there was no reward at the flush. The season was closed and I carried no gun, just the clean moral sword of the do-gooder. That doesn't kill many quail.

Further, there was neither high-grading of cover nor skirting abysmal places. A transect takes none of that into account. It is laid out on an aerial photo, translated to the ground by flagged stakes and going from Point A to Point B without deviation—as does the stumbling researcher. There were ditches, fences, and creeks in our path, but aside from absolutely unavoidable detours we walked the literal straight and narrow.

We crossed good habitat and bad—across cut cornfields and empty meadows. The idea was to see how efficiently bird dogs can find available quail. Two of the research team wore earphones and carried equipment that looked like it was stolen from Channel Nine Action News. The team played a game of Fake Out—we never knew if they were triangulating a real covey or an imaginary one, so we couldn't use their position as a clue to direct the dogs. Even the biologists, Tom Dailey and John Schulz, didn't know if the telemetry team was faking or not.

The multiyear study, which wound up in 1996, taught us more about Missouri's favorite game bird than anyone had ever known, and the implications are as important for hunters as they are for quail managers.

Where do quail roost? And when and why? How many quail do hunters take from what's available? How many do predators take? When and why? How do quail respond to the presence of a dog?

The questions are endless—and so are the transects, if you happen to be walking them. Six or seven miles of daily hiking wasn't unusual.

Blind Pony Lake bisects the wildlife area. The east side was open to statewide hunting regulations, while the west side was restricted—hunting by drawing only and a short season.

Hunters took far fewer birds on the west side and more quail survived the winter, but by nesting time the populations were roughly equal on both sides of the lake. Dailey was surprised by how many birds hunters took under statewide regulations: more than 70 percent the first year of the study and more than 80 percent the second.

Quail managers have maintained for years that hunting is "compensatory," not "additive." In simpler terms, if hunters don't get a quail, something else will. One study doesn't prove the theory, but it's a strong indicator that hunting doesn't add to the perils a quail faces—it just substitutes for something else.

Yet another discovery: People may think they invented house-husbands, but quail have been doing it forever. Thanks to the transmitters, Dailey has found that male quail incubate eggs about 25 percent of the time.

"Quail are quite promiscuous," he says. "We always thought that they were monogamous, that a hen and cock got together and raised a brood, but we've found that a hen will lay a clutch of eggs, then go off to find another male while the first male takes over incubation."

That's one reason a low quail population can rebound so quickly.

The study involved not only professionals but also volunteers with bird dogs that ranged from so-so (someone else's dogs) to wonderful (my dogs). We let the dogs range pretty much at will, but generally back and forth across the transect line.

On the average, the dogs found about 50 percent of the available birds. "Average" implies that some dogs couldn't find quail stapled to the ends of their noses, while others pretty well swept the place clean. The success ratios ranged from a low of 17 percent (that's the hunter trying to sell his dog) to a high of 71 percent (the hunter who wouldn't take a million dollars for Rounder).

Schulz and Dailey measured humidity, wind speed, and a flock of variables, all of which went into a computer that spit out information on how well bird dogs do under given weather conditions (and where birds are likely to be under the same conditions).

There is endless potential here. Knowing where quail tend to be in, say, terrible weather provides an indication of what to plant to provide quail food and shelter for terrible weather (and also where to hunt).

Blind Pony manager Jerry Hamilton, a fisheries man by profession and a quail hunter by inclination, has turned the 2,207-acre wildlife area into a quail hunter's delight. Even so, quail numbers were substantially down in 1995-96, including in the the area where regulations strictly limited the kill. And that would indicate that no matter how tenderly you treat your bird crop, there can be busts.

Nasty spring weather crippled the quail hatch. Perhaps other factors came into play (including, possibly, disruption from the researchers themselves).

Hamilton tries to work over a third of the area every year, desprouting old fields, planting lespedeza, maintaining warm-season grass plots, cropping, planting food plots—if it's good for quail, you'll find it at Blind Pony. They call it "disturbing" ground—sprouting, discing, and the like. Quail thrive where there are annual seed-bearing plants and old-field cover.

Missouri's three-year study was supposed to be duplicated in six states, but money and other problems have interfered, so there's no telling when the other studies will corroborate, contradict, or amplify the Missouri findings. But findings alone are no guarantee of improved hunting.

Missouri had suffered several sub-par seasons through the mid-1990s. Wet springs in 1993 and 1995 certainly affected nesting. And habitat continues to decline as the small family farms become big corporate operations with clean fencerows and fall-plowed fields.

Fescue, a wildlife abomination, now makes up most of Missouri's pastureland (in the 1940s it was essentially absent, and most Missouri hay and pastureland was in legumes, good for quail).

Maybe there are other factors, but quail hunting simply isn't as good as it was in the glory days of the late 1960s (when there were about three times as many quail hunters). I'd like to be optimistic about the future of quail hunting, but with almost all bobwhite states in decline, it's tough to do.

As you might expect, hunting is best earlier in the season. One season I found five coveys in an hour on a public wildlife area. A week later I didn't turn up a single bird on the same walk. Many hunters would say that area was "shot out" or the birds had been harassed and driven somewhere else. But on subsequent hunts I found some of those missing coveys—and I also hunted all the "somewhere elses" and didn't find birds. They were there; I just didn't find them.

As an interesting sidelight to the research that says early-season hunting is best, I've often had my best hunts the last week of the season, including last season, when my son and I found five coveys in three hours and limited out.

That same walk on two earlier hunts hadn't produced a bird. Where were they?

While the smartest bird isn't much brighter than a rock, quail do quickly learn to avoid the gun. I've hunted a covey for years that lurks along a river. Obviously, with an estimated 70–90 percent annual mortality, the birds aren't the same from year to year—but their habits are.

I doubt it's genetic, but whether genetic or behavior passed from generation to generation, the birds invariably flush across the river, even if you try to cut them off. They'll fly through you if they have to. That is their escape route, and it serves them well, because unless you want to swim in November and December you aren't going to follow them.

That covey, no matter how hard it is hunted by however many hunters, will have two-thirds of its members intact when the season closes. Happens every year. The few birds that don't fly the river make up the third of the covey that doesn't survive.

I KNOW HUNTERS who rarely miss. If the limit is eight, they'll limit out with less than a dozen shots. Part of it is restraint—resisting the urge to salute birds out of range or that offer little chance of success. Part is shooting skill, much of which is a quick mount of the gun followed by deliberate shooting.

Check yourself out: In Florida, a study of 6,820 shots found that it took 3.1 shots to bag a quail. In other words, if you can shoot an eight-bird limit in a box of shells, you're average.

I was told that Nash Buckingham, the legendary outdoor writer and by all accounts a fine shotgunner, preached in his inimitable southern accent, "Suh, you must learn the art of restraint." Another hunter recommends counting to three before shooting. Easy to say, difficult to do.

In most areas, hunters consider finding a covey an hour excellent hunting, which translates to a six- or seven-covey day (unless you have more stamina than I have). But in a good year in Texas, where the bobwhite is King Bird, and on some of those southern plantations where Mr. Buck and Archibald Rutledge hunted and where you and I won't, hunters routinely put up fourteen to twenty coveys a day.

There may be three or more quail per acre on those places. I'm lucky to find a place with a quail to two acres. Of course, they aren't scattered like that; there'd be one twelve-bird covey on twenty-four acres.

Quail hunting can be wearying, frustrating, and unproductive, but it's always the season to which the rest of the year points.

And no matter how worn down I am at the end of it, I'm sad when the last day comes, knowing that there are a scattered few seasons in a person's life, and they come and go with increasing speed.

I've turned sixty-two, a watershed no one likes to cross. Forty is an age when they joke about you being over the hill, but you still stay out late and pop up early and do all the things you used to, only with a few more aches. Fifty is just getting into the swing. I was still playing my teenage son one-on-one in basketball at fifty and beating him once in a while.

But sixty? Sixty is verging on old, and old is for old people. Part of growing old is attitude, and if that were all of it I'd have acne and a breaking voice the rest of my life. But you can't escape eroded cartilage and ligament lassitude forever. What used to be a seven-hour day now is often five, and I feel it more. After two or three straight days of hunting I'm ready to spend one reading a book or contemplating my navel. Still, five hours in the quail fields is a pretty good day, and I cover plenty of miles. I'm not what I once was, but what I am is preferable to the alternative.

So the dogs and the hunters grow older, and none will reclaim the vigor of youth. We have our memories and our tears. The sweet face of the Brittany I am looking at as I write this will be a memory some day.

Another will always be there to contribute—not to replace, for no creature can become another, but to create a new set of memories as sweet as those of the one that's gone. I could not be without a hunting dog, a companion of the many fields and the many miles. While the old one grows old the young one capers and wonders, not realizing it is waiting its turn and that there is another somewhere behind, perhaps not even born.

I don't mean to be maudlin, for quail hunting has been a very happy part of a very happy life. There wasn't much intense drama. Quail hunting is not like stalking grizzly bears or going after wounded rhino in the bush.

I guess the most dangerous quail-hunting experience I've ever had was wrecking my Suburban one night on the way back to a motel. I started an endless skid at forty-five miles an hour when I hit ice that I didn't know was there.

I slid sideways down the highway, clipped a bridge sign that spun the vehicle more than 360 degrees (and saved it from plunging ten feet into deep, icy water). The Burb then dove off the other end of the bridge, again just missing the plunge into the creek, and sailed down a steep embankment into a foot of water, mud, and snow.

Nothing even moved inside, including two dog carriers with four dogs, who, wide-eyed, peered out through the ventilation holes as if wondering what in God's name the boss was doing now.

My hunting diary entry for that evening was shaky and dealt more with the need for thanks than with my hunting.

I have a dim memory of falling through the ice once when I was barely adolescent. I think I was carrying a gun, had no dog, and was perhaps a mile from the farmhouse. It was about twenty degrees, and I if I hadn't drowned I could have frozen. But I did neither. I struggled out of the creek and ran for the house as my clothing froze and my skin numbed. It took a long time to warm up, but there was no damage done, and as a traumatic memory it doesn't amount to much—so dim that I don't remember the details.

I still have flashbacks to the wreck, however, and shudder as if a great Suburban had driven over my grave. Perhaps it made me appreciate quail hunting more, and there's no doubt it made me appreciate Chevrolet and life a *whole* lot more.

ELEMENTAL TO THE DIVISION between hunters and antihunters is the concept of killing for sport. There is no resolution to that—people believe what they believe, and if someone thinks it's wrong or immoral to kill for sport I have no quarrel. If nothing else, it lessens the competition. I do object to others trying to prevent me from hunting just because they think it's wrong.

Historically, those who try to impose moral values have caused more trouble than any other group. Fanatics act fanatically.

On the other hand, people have a perfect right under our system to seek redress under the law, and if they can get hunting banned I'll have to live with it or move somewhere hunting is legal. It's hypocritical of me both to endorse legislation that proscribes a farmer from certain actions on his land (conversion of wetlands, for example) and to argue against antihunters trying to ban hunting.

I just hope legislators recognize that activity vindicated by time is legitimate and that a ban on hunting is an invitation to other groups seeking to ban any human activity with which they don't agree—ranging from pornography (under their definition, of course) to Sunday sports. Book banning or burning is only a small step away when legislators and zealots join forces.

Beyond the moral issue of hunting is another basic issue. It may even underlie and explain the stand taken by antihunters:

our concept that the individual has worth. We need to believe that to justify our existence. It's frightening to think we're just another quail in the covey, food for fate. We need to be something special or we face chaos. Quail don't ratiocinate. They're content to be a cog in the roosting wheel, but we aren't.

We cherish our existence: A person's pride is his treasure. We hold the apparent randomness of existence at bay by believing in our unique value. We could have been born on the mean streets of India or among the teeming masses in Bangladesh instead of being a well-fed someone reading a sporting book in a comfortable chair, with no threat larger than an IRS audit to mar the known future.

If people lose faith in their personal value, then they have lost their reason for life. But the biologist realizes (or should) that the individual is meaningless in nature; the species is all-important. That simple idea is anathema to the antihunter. He or she sees only the bloody individual, limp in death, and is horrified.

It is akin to the poet John Donne's famous line "Any man's death diminishes me." So does the antihunter feel diminished by the hunter-caused death of a deer or duck.

Individuals become important in wildlife management only if the population declines to a point where individuals *are* important—whooping cranes or trumpeter swans or any endangered species.

To a caring biologist, it's foolish to spend great sums of money to rescue a few individual animals caught in an oil spill or even trapped by nature, as three whales were a few years back when Arctic ice closed in around them.

The whole world rallied to save those whales. God knows what the effort cost, but the same amount could have been applied to whale management or research and done a hell of a lot more good for the species. The same media that wept over the whales ignores the less personal story of a species in trouble because of the inexorable erosion of habitat.

Antihunters use a shotgun approach, and, as I do with quail, sometimes they hit something. For example, there is much to be said for the antihunting argument that wildlife managers tinker with habitat to create targets for hunters. It is true that some habitat manipulation is for the benefit of a shootable species, with deer a prime example.

I feel virtuous being a quail hunter because quail-habitat management is perhaps the most ideal for all wildlife species. Take a field and divide it into strips of crops alternated with legumes and woody cover and you have created an area in which the majority of wildlife will thrive, both hunted and nonhunted.

True, deep woodland birds may be at a disadvantage, but in nature a mature forest is a specialized ecosystem where few species thrive. The counterargument is that there isn't much mature forest and therefore there are few of its residents, while there is much farm and second-growth habitat.

BUT GENERALLY, the arguments of the antihunting crowd show an alarming ignorance of life as it really is. What bothers me more than hearing some glitzy movie star spouting idiocies is the gawp-jawed acceptance the audience gives her. Are people so damn dumb that they believe everything an actor says just because he or she can convincingly mouth the words of a scriptwriter who likewise doesn't know the score?

I confess I'm baffled by the intricacies of life, so much so that it's easier not to think about it or, like Scarlett O'Hara, to think about it tomorrow. For example, animal-rights activists are horrified by the use of animals in laboratory research, and it is disturbing to think of primates or dogs or guinea pigs being subjected to pain.

Lab animals likely don't reason the way humans do and so are spared the agony of suspense and hopelessness—but they still feel pain and apprehension and are deprived of their freedom, even if they don't know it on an intellectual level. It's easy to transfer the empathy for an unknown lab dog to your bird dog and feel horror at the thought of Spike or Belle under the researcher's knife.

But life is full of inequality. A dog can be born to hunt and be cherished and loved and have a full, rich life, or it can be a starving mutt in an alley or a traumatized dog in a laboratory. And a person can be a quail hunter with fifty years of rich rambles in golden fields or he can be covered with festering sores, dying of starvation in a Bombay ghetto.

It's all a matter of chance. There are people richer than me, poorer, sicker, healthier, better-looking, uglier. I hunt with better bird dogs than mine and worse. So I can't accept the argument that society should take care of animals as if the world were one great welfare society. We must devise guidelines for our behavior, but they must be practical guidelines. It is not practical to guarantee a full and untroubled life to every person, nor is it practical to do so for animals.

I don't subscribe to the biblical assertion that man has dominion over all the animals. I think we're just another animal with the same biological imperatives as squirrels and rabbits. I do believe that, because we have power and intellect, we should treat animalkind well. But I also feel that some animals exist to be food for others. To deny that is to deny ourselves.

The world breaks down into predators and prey, and we are predators. Sport hunting is an extension of hunting for food. Most game is consumed, either by the hunter or by someone he gives it to. The fact that the hunter enjoys the contest is immaterial. That's a bone stuck in the throat for the antihunter, but I have no sympathy for that.

The antihunter who says, "You shouldn't kill animals, and especially you shouldn't kill for sport," might as well say, "You shouldn't call it work if you enjoy what you do, and if you enjoy it, you aren't entitled to pay."

I hunt for the pleasure, but much of the pleasure is in eating the birds and other game I shoot. There are many reasons: Game is largely devoid of contamination (although our chemical farms are doing their best to change that); it is leaner and thus better for my body; properly prepared, game tastes far better than the sterile, bland meat raised under production-line conditions. A game dinner should be a ceremony, both of eating and as a resolution to the hunt.

QUAIL ARE MY LOVE—have been since my father moved back to the farm from the city in 1948. If I were limited to one outdoor pursuit, I would sacrifice fishing, canoeing, turkey hunting, deer hunting, if only I could continue to walk the long birdfields of autumn with my friends and with my dogs.

I'm in good company. Most of the great outdoor writers have been bird men. Ray Holland said, "I have seen the best of dogs blunder into birds through no fault of theirs." Holland said he'd rather have a dog with brains and a mediocre nose than "a keen nosed dog that was shy on think power."

Nash Buckingham, the elder statesman of quail-hunting writers, said, "Too many dogs along are worse than none." He summed up what makes a good quail dog: "It requires bobwhites, continual contacts with them, and patient work, to shape any pointer's or setter's true destiny."

"Sometimes a dog points because he's a jolly good fellow," says Charley Dickey, who once quoted Shakespeare at the head of a chapter on quail dogs: "He hath eaten me out of house and home," and at the beginning of a discussion on each major breed: "His better doth not breathe upon the earth."

Havilah Babcock, the dean of quail writers, said, "Seven ounces of avoirdupois could be wrapped up in no other shape or form that would possess such power to befog and confound the senses or to disconcert and disorganize the human nervous system." He also wrote, "Bird hunting gets into a man's blood worse than the seven-year itch. I've never known a bird hunter to quit. They die sometimes, but never quit."

Tom Huggler, whose book *Quail Hunting in America* (Stackpole, 1987) is the standard reference available today, said, "There is more to hunting quail than reducing the bird to a gamebag statistic."

They're all wrestling with the magic of Bird, none quite pinning it down. Yes, there is more to quail hunting than statistics. But what exactly, you may ask.

What is the power of a sunset? The definition of love? What is the softness of puppy breath or the feel of a fine shotgun?

Some things you just accept and hope they never go away.

# 2

# GROWING UP BOBWHITE

THE SEASON ended the way it began—with a birdless trudge. Many seasons have ended that way recently. Nationally, our quail hunting is not what it once was. But in between opening and ending were a few good hunts, a bunch of frustrating ones, some fair shooting, and much terrible shooting.

Forty-seven birds, that's all. I know hunters who kill two hundred a year, but they don't often miss and they probably hunt more than I do. I don't know. It seems as if I'm always hunting, at least it used to seem that way to my boss when I had one.

If success is measured by the dead pile, then I'm a flop. Quail shooting should be simple. I once asked a good quail shot what he did, and he said, "I just put the bead on their little feathered butts."

Simple—but so hard to do when their little feathered butts are airborne.

If you measure quail success by miles walked, then I'm rich. I'm rich in bruises and sprains and scratches, in arches threatening to tumble, in ankles that wobble and knees that creak.

I can't help quail hunting any more than someone infatuated can help doing silly things like hiring sky writers to spell out "I Love Pammy" in the skies. Maybe I'll find some pilot and get him to write "I Love Quail Hunting" overhead. And the birds will look up in fear that a new mutation of marsh hawk is on the prowl.

I'm verging on my fiftieth year of hunting bobwhite quail. There were a few years off when I thought making a living and establishing a career were more important than chasing birds. What a stupid, immature attitude! Thank goodness I've solved that problem. I took early retirement a few years back, beginning on an October 1, which gave me a few days to get ready for quail season.

I hunted at least three times a week that first season of retirement, and several years later, I still do. My dogs and the guys I bust brush with are my best friends, and our two and a half months together, November through mid-January, are what the year is all about. The rest of the year is thinking about that time.

I've stayed in fleabag motels, camped in deep snow, been soaked through, coated with ice. I've fallen into ditches, strained or sprained nearly every joint, suffered from feet so sore I could barely walk, been attacked by crotch-grab that brought me to my knees. I've ripped every square inch of my skin, gotten poked in the eye, caught colds, flu, intestinal wham-bam, and once had a dangerous case of blood poisoning after I was attacked by a tree.

I've eaten food that street people wouldn't touch. I've broken up dogfights and ridden with a dog who thought she was tougher than a skunk. I've laid dogs to rest and mourned with tears and deep grief, and I've brought puppies along and been filled with joy when they did what it was in their nature to do. I've slept with dogs and deburred them, yelled at them, run them down in

Olympic sprints to administer whippings for forgetting that we were quail hunting.

I've bought expensive shotguns and enough ammo to overthrow the government of a midsized nation. I've dressed birds in the snow until my fingers went numb, and I've bitten so hard on $7\,^1/_2$ shot in lovingly prepared quail that my shriek of agony was matched only by the shriek of joy from my dentist.

I have fought through briars that would have caused Brer Rabbit to apply for Medicare. I have waded rivers in January after a covey that thought it was escaping by flying across. I have been torn on rusty barbed-wire fences and have run horseweed stalks up my nose.

I have been there.

And if Fate isn't hiding in the bushes with one of his practical jokes, I'll be out there again next November 1, perhaps not finding any birds again but with the fond expectation that I will.

You see, the bird hunter always knows he will limit, the dogs will perform flawlessly, his shooting will be near 100 percent. He is the eternal optimist, and the evidence of the past means nothing. We quail hunters are like nations. We don't learn from our mistakes.

The only creature more optimistic than a bird hunter is the dog whose butt end he pursues. The dogs know they will find birds every time out. No real bird dog sulks in the kennel when you appear in brush pants. Instead, he or she goes bananas, leaping, yipping with gee-whiz enthusiasm. My neighbors especially appreciated this and my roared commands to "Shut up!" at 5:30 in the morning, when we were setting out on a long hunting trip.

None of my neighbors, when I had them, hunted quail. They regarded me as a suspicious, possibly dangerous person who rolled around on the ground with a freshet of puppies every so often like a twelve-year-old.

Training a dog to hand signals is a strange occupation, involving violent gestures that look as if the trainer is possessed. Every so often I would see the timid lady next door peering through the curtains, considering whether to dial 911. But we moved to the country and forty acres, where the dogs can chase squirrels and rabbits with unleashed gusto, and I can bawl awful curses that disturb only the neighboring livestock.

The dogs grow older, in bigger chunks than I do. Guff, who was my main dog for a dozen years, caught me in dog years. If, as they say, a dog's year is equivalent to seven of ours, Guff was eighty-four years going on six months when Death, surely a hell of a sprinter, caught up with him.

Guff and I had the same outlook on life. We went at it as if we were driving for a layup. We watched the countryside when driving and evaluated the habitat. If a bird flew, we saw it with predatory interest. I've come close to a few accidents when my car wandered at the same time as did my attention.

Guff and I both liked beautiful females, and we both enjoyed eating. But most of all, we loved to bird hunt together. Neither one of us liked to quit, but we both became more prone to fatigue than we used to be.

I still like beautiful females, whether they're of my species or Guff's, and Tess, my sweet little lady dog, is my girlfriend.

Guff enjoyed watching television with me after the hunt. We sprawled on our backs, him in my arms, disgustingly splayed out. He didn't smell so good, but I probably didn't either, and it didn't much matter.

Once the season is over, it is over. There are those who enter their dogs in competition and play with pen-reared birds that fly like meadowlarks. This is an artificial thing, and I don't do it. It's like donning a tux to eat at McDonald's.

Instead, I herd the dogs into the truck and go to a nearby wildlife area, where I turn them loose in a canine tidal swell and they run wild, out of control, and I don't care. They know the difference between me in orange with a gun and me in a tee shirt with no gun. This is fun time, time to burn calories and jump at butterflies.

Sometimes I practice hand signals or "Whoa!" and they dutifully perform, but we both get tired of it and they go for a swim in the pond and I plink rocks into the water and think about November 1.

I fish for catfish, a Brittany dozing in the sun beside me, and think about quail season. It's ninety-five degrees or more and sweat rolls off me, but if I hold my tongue just right I can feel sleet threatening to turn to snow and see the dog freeze deep in a brushy gully where the birds have gone to get out of the wind. The reverie is interrupted by a hefty bite, and I resent it even as I haul the writhing fish in and clip it to my stringer.

I think about the guys I hunt with who grow gray whiskers and groan a lot as we sprawl in the Foul Air Motel (it used to be the Bon Air, but twenty years of hosting quail hunters has left it slightly redolent of the kennel).

Bobwhite quail were the game creature of choice when I was a kid.

Well, it really wasn't much of a choice. There were no deer or wild turkeys in Chariton County, Missouri. Doves were something you sometimes shot off the wires from the back of a 1946 Ford pickup.

My grandpa shot squirrels, which proliferated in the doomed big woods of the old Chariton River bottom. Doomed because modern farming would move in and clear the towering sycamores and oaks to make way for corn and beans.

Even the river was sacrificed to the Great God Agriculture. The old river wound nearly nine hundred miles from the Iowa line to the Missouri River. It was fish-rich, and its banks were ripe with game.

A huge flood in 1825 wiped out the town of Charaton (settlers, being about as good at spelling as they were at settling, changed the spelling somewhere along the way), a trading post set up by John Charaton. Another flood in 1844 was supposed to have been the worst in history.

Because the old river occasionally let its floodplain settlers know who was boss, the residents decided to jerk it straight and let the floodwaters go down the gut to the Missouri River.

Channelization is a godforsaken crime against nature, but man is prone to perform such blasphemies routinely and only wonder about it later. The Chariton still floods, despite a channelization job that shortened it from nine hundred miles to about one hundred. (In my home county, Chariton, three hundred miles of wonderful old river became thirty-three miles of stinking ditch.)

The 1930s and 1940s were the time of the quail. Family farms were a reality, not the moribund dream seen in agribusiness commercials today. I remember our family farm, but now it is gone. I made one pilgrimage back there on a cold winter day, ostensibly to hunt quail but really to walk the sharp hills and see where I once lived.

Few farmers owned more than three hundred acres back in the 1940s and 1950s, most not near that many. Most farmers, at least in Chariton County, still plowed with horses. The main cash crop was tobacco, with maybe a little corn for livestock consumption. A few raised wheat.

By the time I was old enough to get a take on Chariton County, it was a gullied mess, tobaccoed to death, a thin country of infertile uplands and scrubby trees, except in the bottoms, where the trees were protected by the inhospitality of wet land.

Rural electrification didn't appear until the 1940s, and there were no paved roads. Most farmers were quail hunters, and the pointer was the unanimous dog of choice. All of them looked starved, but then most hardworking pointers do.

The hunters were lean and chewed homegrown and wore overalls and shot humpbacked Browning automatics (or Sears, Roebuck autoloaders). They could put three quail on the ground before I could get my gun to my shoulder.

My first gun was a Stevens 12-gauge single-shot sawed off to about twenty-three inches. I remember that gun the way you remember the bully in grade school who cornered you on the playground and bloodied your nose.

That gun hurt me.

It had an external hammer, and after its truncation it weighed only about four pounds, shot a pattern as wide open as Dakota Territory, and kicked a ten-year-old kid like the Missouri state animal.

I waited more than forty years to go back and see what had happened to the old farm where I'd spent my childhood summers. I knew you really can't go back, but I wanted to see how things had changed.

I remembered the old single-shot as I swung off the blacktop into the driveway and let the dog out. I'd flushed the first quail I ever shot across the road in a brushy gully. I was ten years old, forty-four years before.

The bird was topping the rim of the gully when I fired, and I tumbled backward as the butt slammed into my skinny shoulder and the top lever ripped the webbing between my thumb and forefinger. But the bird was dead in the weeds, still warm and feather-soft in my bloody hand. That was hundreds of quail ago, but that first bird is the most clearly remembered of them all.

I spent summers in the old farmhouse. My aunt and uncle, who lived in the main part of the house, and my grandfather, who had his own three-room annex, lie in the Asbury churchyard, about a half mile up what used to be a gravel road. The steeple is visible through the leaf-bare winter forest.

My pilgrimage took place on the first day of a new year, cold and gray. The last time I had been at the old farmhouse I'd drunk lemonade and listened to cousins, aunts, uncles, and neighbors talk about the war and eat watermelon from Aunt Sis's garden. The war was the long-ago war to end all wars. There have been a couple since, and no one learns anything.

I uncased the L. C. Smith and shoved in a couple of shells. The day was damply chill. The clouds were low to the earth. No one has lived here for years, but a cousin keeps watch over the house, and kids from neighboring farms brush-hog the ridgetops, mostly so they can hunt deer and turkeys. My uncle raised tobacco on a couple of acres, butchered his own livestock for meat, even made lye soap from the rendering. He sprayed his tobacco with Paris Green, an arsenic-based insecticide, and chewed his dried leaves. He died of stomach cancer.

The farm is 160 acres, shaped like an outspread hand, with the house at the wrist, ridges running off like fingers, and wooded slopes between.

I walked to the barn, remembering the time my uncle got into a bottle of liquor he had stashed and came rolling back to the house at suppertime much like the sailor he was in World War I, flushed of face, full of jokes and irrepressible laughter. I figured milking the cows agreed with him, but my aunt knew better.

Lennie, my first girlfriend, lived down the road, and once we sat in the haymow door and watched wasps hang in the still summer heat. I thought I impressed her, a kid from the city, but she told a girlfriend that I was "green."

The barn now is sagging and weathered, doors leaning on single hinges like drunks against a lamppost. I didn't bother to go in. It used to be a cathedral, its roof impossibly high above. Now it's just another rotting old farm building with no one to care.

I passed a pond, dried in Missouri's long drought, where I used to swim with the bullheads, yellow Chariton County clay oozing between my kid toes. The trees and bushes were rimed with frost. Silvered, like my hair, they seemed ghost bushes and trees, maybe memories from long ago.

I moved on into the back pasture, which should have been long and open. I used to ride a bicycle here at breakneck speed, terrorizing the livestock. But now the pasture is narrow and clogged with brush, and before long I was at a wooded bluff that overlooked a road I'd never seen. There shouldn't have been a road, but as if to prove me wrong a modern car passed below me.

Maybe it's the old road that goes down to the Chariton River crossing. There was a hardware store at the bridge, where my father bought me a Daisy Red Ryder BB gun.

The Guilfords lived up the hill. Once I saw one of the Guilford girls, on whom I had a mild crush, running through the yard in her underwear. It was a magic moment. She would be more than sixty years old now.

I don't know what happened to the BB gun, but we used to have wars with them, despite our mothers' warnings that "you'll shoot your eyes out." I actually did get hit in the eye once, but it did no damage.

There've been Vances on this ridge for a long time. Joseph Vance settled in the forks of the Chariton River in 1818, and he and the other early settlers, the Dinsmores and Hayses, were plagued by Indians but persevered. Nearly a century and a half later I went to school with both Dinsmores and Hayses and never saw an Indian.

Roy Joe, my cousin, was born in this house, grew up there as a lanky, jug-eared Missouri kid, joined the paratroops in World War Two, parachuted into Normandy on D-day, broke his back on landing, and fought for five days behind the German lines because he really didn't have a choice.

Life in the Chariton River hills always has been tough. Kids learned to survive or they just didn't. Diphtheria visited many families and influenza stalked others. But it wasn't just disease.

My father and his brother were fooling around with a .22 one day, and my uncle Sam shot my father in the lower lip with a .22 short. More afraid of their mother than of medical consequences, they somehow conspired to keep her from knowing what had happened, and my father carried the little chunk of lead with him the rest of his life.

There is photo of the two of them at about the age I was when I lived on the farm. Tom and Huck would have howdied them and challenged them to a game of aggies.

I passed a pile of deer droppings, something I never would have seen in the 1940s. There were no deer then in Chariton County. Quail, squirrels, rabbits, but no deer and no turkeys. It was a notable event when my father saw his first deer in the 1950s, a grown man with a grown son.

But even without big game it was hunter's country. Small game flourished, and I see now with a grandfather's eyes why this rough, tired hill country appealed to my grandfather.

He was a one-eyed old predator when I knew him, with a bushy mustache, lean as only a hill rover can be. A billet flew up and hit him in the face when he was splitting wood and put one eye out. But the eye that remained was that of a goshawk, and the squirrel in the sights of his Marlin bolt-action .22 was tonight's supper.

In his eighties he still strode over the ridges to the Chariton River, where he had set fish traps as exquisitely crafted as they were illegal. His name was Joseph and he was a carpenter, but there wasn't much biblical about his legacy to me.

He left me a fierce desire to hunt, and that's really what I was doing on that cold January first. Revisiting my childhood home, yes, but also looking for a covey of quail.

The woods were soundless, almost spooky in their repose. But then there was an explosion of wings on the next ridgetop and a large flock of turkeys scattered. The only turkey hereabouts when I was a kid was an enormous domestic tom who terrorized me. I hated that aggressive, righteously stupid bully, and when he became Sunday dinner I relished every bite of him with spiteful glee.

Guff, who had pointed these super quail from time to time, was transfixed by the turkeys. The place was a no-man's-land of briar and bramble, wild rose, blackberry, and locust. I cussed when a rose thorn speared through my brush pants and into my leg.

How different I was from the kid with the bruised shoulder of forty-five years ago. He wore ratty sneakers, tattered blue jeans, and a ripped shirt and carried a few paper shotshells in his pants pocket for the rusty single-shot Stevens.

I wore Thinsulate-insulated, Gore-Tex-waterproofed boots with Vibram soles, Cordura-faced brush pants, a Royal Robbins shirt, and a Bob Allen shell vest and carried a valuable L. C. Smith double-barrel, loaded with Winchester's newest and highest-priced field loads. Save for the obvious wear on all this stuff and on me, I could have posed for a Yuppie catalog.

We were light-years apart, that kid and me, except in attitude; that was the same—we'd rather be walking those weary ridges than doing anything else. He'd skip school to do it; I would skip work. We both go it alone by preference. Neither of us ever learned to shoot very well, but we always think we will.

I really didn't expect to find quail. I knew much better places than that old briar patch. I'd have been satisfied with one covey and maybe one bird, but I had nearly looped the fingered ridges back to the barn without any action.

Two deer spooked out of a hollow and bounded up the far ridge. They stopped and dropped their tails and instantly vanished into the bleak gray hillside. I exhaled, and they started running again, over the hill. Shortly I spotted an antler under a rosebush. It was half of a massive ten-point rack, with long, burnished tines that, if the other half were identical, would qualify the owner for Boone and Crockett listing. Some time later I found another antler, partly gnawed by rodents, and figured it was the first of the two to have fallen. Maybe the owner, quietly alert, was watching me prowl his domain.

I was in sight of the barn now, without quite knowing how I got there. Same as old times—my aunt never knew where I was and most of the time I didn't either. But I always managed to find my way out of the woods and to the dinner table.

The dinner table was gone, along with the massive Warm Morning woodstove that heated and cooked for the Finnells. The inside of the house was nearly bare, but there was a box of moldy books and I thumbed through them.

Most were Westerns or crime novels from the 1920s and 1930s. My grandfather had read most of them and written his opinion in each: "This book is good," he said of Jack London's *South Sea Tales*, and he liked James Oliver Curwood's *The River's End*. (He and Curwood shared a middle name, Oliver.)

But there was nothing written in Voltaire's *Candide* or Balzac's *Scenes of Parisian Life*. I doubt he'd read those. Curwood was a hell of a lot closer to Chariton County than the drawing rooms of old Paris.

We had homemade biscuits every morning, with grape jelly or plum preserves from fruit that grew just outside the house. These biscuits didn't come in a can from the supermarket. They came from flour and shortening and soda and my aunt's rolling pin and biscuit cutter. They tasted like Heaven. The honey was from a bee tree, cut in the woodlot across the gravel road when I was so small that memory was a sometime thing.

Once I went with the men in the dark of a winter night and someone handed me a chunk of comb, dripping with honey. I couldn't believe the Big People were encouraging me to eat something so sweet and so good. Mostly they said, "Don't eat sweets. They'll rot your teeth." It was a revelation: The outdoors contained things I liked that also were good for me. Kidhood wasn't twenty-one years of involuntary servitude after all.

There was a noise somewhere in the still house. Ghosts? Probably squirrels. The whole place is a refuge for wildlife now.

I left the house and crossed the road to the gullied brush field where I'd shot the first quail, but it was thickly wooded with no openings. I had forgotten: In forty years, seedlings grow tall.

It was raw and cold and beginning to snow. I turned and looked back at the house, through spits of snow that wet my face. Something wet my face anyway.

I crossed the road, climbed into the elegant Suburban, pulled out onto the blacktopped highway, and headed south toward the next century.

TWO YEARS LATER I watched the family farm sell on a bitter October day and mourned for a time that cannot come again. The northwest wind nipped leaves off the old maples in the front yard and threw them on the ground for winter to digest.

My father and his brother bought the farm in 1933 and gave their father and mother a piece of land on which to anchor the rest of their lives.

They were selling the place where I first fell in love, learned about fleas and how horses mate, learned to ride a bicycle and play a guitar. I shot my first quail there and listened to Aunt Sade's screeching voice as she told of hearing the guns during the war. She was more than ninety, deaf and loudly boring, but the war she remembered was the Civil War. When I realize that in my lifetime I knew a living link to the Civil War, I also realize that the hourglass doesn't hold much sand at the top.

My first girlfriend lived a quarter mile south, down a bumpy gravel road. My buddy Maurice Young lived where he still does, a quarter mile north. Maurice, his bristly mustache gone gray, tried to buy the place on that cold day, bidding against a stranger in a cowboy hat. Maurice wanted the farm for his son. Maurice is related to me somehow. There are Youngs way back in the Vance family, and almost everyone in those old hills is related somehow. Had he bought it, the place still would be in the family.

But he didn't.

"Your folks used to come up to my place and borrow my cradle when you was a baby," said an elderly man, one of the Meyerses, as we wiped at our drizzling noses. "You'd sleep there when you was visitin'." I didn't remember.

We watched like spectators at a tennis match as Maurice and the cowboy lobbed bids back and forth. At the end, even though Maurice had deeper roots in the thin hill soil, the stranger had deeper pockets.

Maurice is family. The guy in the cowboy hat? Who the hell knows. Just a cowboy with mean eyes and enough money to buy someone else's life.

Couldn't be helped. "We're all getting *old*, Joel!" said one cousin. She's eighty. The youngest is nearly seventy. None of their kids wanted the place, at least not enough to plunk down $104,000 for sentiment. But no one in the family really wanted it sold either. They were raised there. They saw one another get courted, get married, go off to war. The cousins were bent not so much by the years as by the weight of what they were doing.

It didn't take long to erase sixty years of family history. A few minutes and the place went to the stranger in the cowboy hat.

The L-shaped house had grown more ramshackle since I was there with Guff and probably is fated for destruction. People I loved lived and died there. My grandpa's little suite of rooms, tacked onto the main house, would go along with the rest of it. And his spirit, if there is such a thing, would go into limbo.

"One time some men came to the farm to quail hunt," Maurice says. "They asked your grandpa Joe to go with them. He got out an old long-barreled single-shot shotgun. Probably had to knock the mud daubers out of it. They felt sorry for him. He only had one eye and that ratty old gun. So they told him he'd get the first shot when the quail got up.

"Well, he not only got the first shot; he got the last one, too." Maurice says. "Covey got up and, *boom!* he powdered one, reloaded, and shot another one before they got out of range. They'd never seen anyone shoot quail like that."

MY UNCLE ROY Finnell added a chunk of land to the home place and moved his big family there. His children are the cousins who were selling the home place. Uncle Finney bought out my dad and uncle back in the 1950s. Otherwise I would have been huddled in the doorway with them, watching my life be juggled by strangers.

The auctioneer prattled the terms of the sale, trying to generate interest in people who mostly were just cold. The windchill was below twenty degrees. I scuffled through the swirling leaves beneath two huge old maples. They'd been huge and old when I was a kid; they still were.

My Aunt Sis's garden had gone to saplings and weeds. One of the cousins had dug some peonies from the yard. With any luck they'd grow for another sixty years, patiently sprouting and hanging in there.

The big old tobacco barn didn't seem as big now. It showed its age with sagging doors and missing boards. Maurice, sharecropping the place, had hung sticks of tobacco in the center section. The broad leaves still were damp and green in spots.

Tobacco was the farm crop when I was a kid. Lucky Strike Green had gone to war, so we raised tobacco for the Boys Over There. It was downright patriotic. What was a soldier without his smoke?

Anything else grown on that farm was environmentally sound. No additives to the chicken or pig food. The pigs ate slops from the kitchen, and the chickens ate what they could find in the yard.

It was a quintessential family farm.

We mourn the loss of the family farm as if it were a bucolic Camelot. Politicians with country constituencies do it routinely, meanwhile getting elected with a pocketful of agribusiness money. There is no room in today's world for a subsistence farm where pigs feed on slop and you make your soap from their rendered lard. No one wants to live that way anyway. Only poor people use homemade soap, and raw milk is dangerous.

We, in our comfortable ignorance, sigh for what was often a thin, mean life. People, especially kids, died of diseases that are only historical curiosities today: diphtheria, whooping cough, scarlet fever.

The Finnells and Vances were poor people. They didn't think of themselves that way, but they lived far below the poverty line as we define it today. They worked from, as a friend says, "can't see to can't see." That's all they did. Work. They raised pigs to eat and smoked the hams and bacon. The smell from the smokehouse on a cold winter day was mouthwatering. Chickens were free to roam until my aunt's culinary eye settled on a luckless victim, and then she planted a substantial foot on its neck and jerked upward on its feet and it was history. Food was plentiful. No one ever went hungry, but they made do with old clothing. New shoes were as rare as an eclipse. A night out was a pie supper at the nearby Asbury Church once or twice a year.

The romance of the family farm? There was nothing romantic in a midnight trek to the outhouse in December with a case of what used to be called the back-door trots. In summer, they shared the outhouse with ill-tempered stinging insects: wasps, yellow jackets, and the occasional sociopathic bumblebee.

My kinfolk spent much of the summer cutting firewood by hand—there were no chainsaws then—and the house, insulated about a quarter as well as today's houses, lost heat as soon as the fire in the stove burned low. It wouldn't get warm until someone got up, well before dawn, and built a fire.

Stereo-in-cab tractors may be overkill, but they beat a team of indifferent horses and a walking plow. Even a riding mower was no picnic. The iron wheels felt square. No one had a sunshade. You endured heat and bugs and dust and sweat. There were no hay balers. You pitched it with a fork atop a horse-drawn wagon. It smelled good but stuck to your sweaty body.

Some opted to leave for the city, as my father and his brother did in the 1920s. They didn't know if Chicago would be easier than Chariton County, but they figured it couldn't be tougher.

My uncle Sam once was asleep in his Chicago apartment when a bullet came through the window and lodged in the wall just above his head. Bullets often flew in Chicago's streets, but they did back on the farm, too, as in the case of the errant .22 bullet my father carried in his lip all his life.

Sis and Finney's kids also chose different paths. None farmed, nor ever wanted to. Roy Joe, the veteran of Normandy, married an English war bride and became an urbanite. Now, fifty years later, he is stooped and gray-haired, more than seventy, a kindly person bitten by the harsh wind.

The guy in the green athletic jacket and the cowboy hat wanted the place. He topped Maurice's bids without hesitation. Maurice chewed on his bids like tough meat, finally being coerced into yet another five-hundred-dollar raise by the impatient auctioneer (who had another farm to sell as soon as he settled this one).

Finally the auctioneer knocked the place down to the cowboy and Maurice shrugged his shoulders philosophically in the cold wind and said, "I gotta spend this afternoon on a tractor and I'm not looking forward to it."

I looked at the cowboy, who glowered at the crowd as if afraid they'd deny him his hard-won prize.

"Come see us," said the cousins. "If you're ever in town, come see us."

I promised I would and maybe I will, but I know only one thing for certain. I'll never again stand beneath the maples, knowing that my taproots grow deep on this old ridge. And I'll never again lie in fresh-mown hay and dream of days to come with my first girlfriend or hold life's first quail, still warm, and know the reality of tomorrow.

# 3

# DAYS ON THE MUSSEL FORK

**WHEN I WAS A KID,** we quail hunted without a bird dog. None of us could afford a dog except Foster, and his was . . . well, to be charitable, a marginal bird dog.

Foster Sadler was my best friend from the moment we met, though he didn't know it for a while. When I was in the eighth grade, my parents moved from Chicago to Dalton, Missouri, and I went through high school at Keytesville. Keytesville was to Dalton as New York City is to . . . well, I'd say Westchester, except I understand Westchester doesn't have dirt streets and poor people.

Foster's dad was the superintendent and Foster was the bright-
est kid in school, lanky with a country face, all angular planes.
We began to hunt together in high school, and save for military
interruptions, we did so for more than thirty years. Foster had
an inquisitive mind and a yen to try new things. He got me interested not only in quail hunting but also in canoeing, skiing, caving, backpacking, bicycling, turkey hunting, deer hunting, and a
host of other activities that I might have tried without him, but
possibly not.

We traveled together over the country to hunt, hike, or fish,
and we camped beneath stars and storms, snow and sunshine. We
even camped a weekend in his parents' back pasture, serenaded
by apprehensive cows. I have no idea now why we camped there,
except it was something to do. Foster's father grumbled, "Can't
understand why anyone would want to sleep on the damn ground
when he's got a nice house."

Joe was the bird dog of marginal repute, a pointer with a yen
for open space. "Goddamit Joe! Get out of the road! Anybody
can hunt the damn road!" Mr. Sadler would bellow at his dog.
Joe would slink into the brush for a few moments, then pop back
onto the gravel road for some easy travelin'. Mr. Sadler's erup-
tions were more traumatic for me than they were for the dog. The
dog paid no attention to him, but I invariably thought he was
yelling at me, the way he did in basketball practice: "Joe, you cut
your head in! You can't shoot right-handed. Why do you want to
shoot left-handed?"

I never quite understood the literal meaning of "cut your head
in," but the figurative one was unmistakable. Either one's head
was cut in or one's ass was on the bench. So the pointer and I
skulked around like a couple of sheep killers, and this took some
of the fun out of quail hunting.

Mickey also was a pointer, but with far more moxie than Joe.
He was Foster's first bird dog after Foster was grown. Mickey had
a funny gait, as if his muscles were screwed on too tight. You
couldn't dent him. He could run all day at top speed and never

stop to pant. When Foster and I dragged back to the car, our legs leaden and breath ragged, Mickey was still loping along with his Groucho Marx gait, ever alert for the elusive scent of quail, rabbits, or possums.

Mickey had a nose that could sniff birds in the next county. Unfortunately, that's often where he hunted. He was a perfect bird dog if you had him in view. I guess he figured if he could see you, you could see him, along with anything he did, so he was on his good behavior.

But let him top a hill, out of sight, and the shackles fell free. Mickey then was his own dog, free to hunt whatever moved. We'd hear him bark in delight as yet another covey went up unseen. What could we do?

Today's trainer is armed with electronic marvels that can reach out and touch a dog a quarter mile away. But a five-hundred-dollar shock collar was as remote to us (even if it had existed) in those far-off days as was a convertible full of lovely and compliant young women.

Without Mickey, we'd find few birds; with him, we found many but missed seeing far more. Mickey was a mixed blessing. Mickey had a not-so-secret ambition to be a lapdog, and at any imagined invitation would crawl into Foster's or my lap. It was like cradling a concrete block. Mickey finally lost a head-butting contest with a cement truck one night, and the world was a little poorer.

Mostly we hunted the Mussel Fork farm, several hundred acres in north Missouri that belonged to Foster's grandparents. Once we turned up fourteen coveys in a day's hunting. This is average on some Texas ranches where quail hunting is a religion, and it once was fairly common in the South, long a bastion of Bird. Now most southern states have so little quail habitat that quail should be on the state threatened list.

In Missouri, near the northern limit of quail range, a fourteen-covey day lingers in the memory for a lifetime. We figure a covey an hour is excellent hunting, and no one hunts fourteen hours a day. So fourteen coveys equal two coveys an hour.

Our hunting wasn't always that good, but it always produced. The land was a mixture of timbered uplands pocked with old fields, and the bottom, which was bisected by the Mussel Fork. The bottom fields were fairly small, lined by brushy fencerows and by the occasional brushy gully.

Good habitat for quail.

Farmers didn't plow in the fall. They left their crop residue, which provided food as well as a bit of cover. The crops were soybeans and corn. Corn is considered a "hot" food, rich in nutrients to carry a quail through hard times. Soybeans aren't as nutritious for the birds, but they are a favored food. Either is far better than nothing.

Sometimes we had good dogs, when someone who owned one would bring it; most of the time we had fair dogs, which stumbled into as many coveys as they pointed.

Once my dog pointed at a groundhog hole and we ridiculed it. The animal rolled its eyes but remained on point, trembling. A fellow hunter got into the narrow ditch to kick around and a quail burst from the hole and flew between my legs as he swung toward it. "Don't shoot!" I screamed, clawing protectively at my shriveling privates.

"Jeez," he grumbled. "I could have gotten it with the second barrel after I blew you out of the way with the first one."

We stayed in a rambling old farmhouse atop a shallow hill. The house had belonged to Foster's grandparents, but they had moved to town and the house was vacant. An oil-burning stove provided heat of sorts. The floor was linoleum, cracked and seamed. The couch near the stove was lumpy and narrow, but I slept there most nights, so tired that the lumps might as well have been goose-down fluff.

Once I got there before Foster, but after dark. I unrolled my sleeping bag and tried to get comfortable on the bulging couch. The old house creaked and mumbled in its restless sleep, and I lay awake wishing I had company. I don't believe in ghosts—sort of—but it would have been nice to have company. Live company.

Then the sky lit up outside, as if dawn had exploded into full day. I sat up startled. The glow quickly faded and died and I pulled on my pants and went outside on the porch.

The night was dark and still, just as it had been before. But there was a faint glow to the north, and I decided something had caught fire. I finished dressing, left the ghosts behind, and drove north on the gravel road. Whatever was afire couldn't be too far away, and perhaps I could help.

I drove for a half hour without getting any closer to the faint glow, and finally I turned around. The next morning I heard a pipeline had exploded and burned in Iowa, more than a hundred miles away.

We learned to hunt quail on those farms. Most of the lessons were simple: First, find good quail habitat. Then walk farther, longer than other hunters. That pretty well sums up the framework of quail hunting.

We learned to hunt woody draws from the thick base to the thin point so we could push birds into the open rather than into the timber. We learned to hunt both sides of the Mussel Fork because quail invariably used the little river as an escape. There were times we'd bounce a covey back and forth across the river, like a tennis ball crossing the net during an extended volley.

A few times when quail populations were down, we'd get up early and perch on the ridge above the Mussel Fork at sunrise and listen for quail whistling their assembly call.

We learned never to pass up an abandoned farmstead, because there's almost always a house covey or a barn covey, usually in the tall horseweeds where the pigs used to live. The old farmsteads have what quail need: cover and food. And perhaps there is a historic affinity between quail and those who work the land.

Almost any old-time farmer will have a barn covey, a bevy of familiar visitors. "You go ahead and hunt," he'll say. "But don't get into my barn covey."

We learned to hunt through the small woodlots when the birds weren't in the traditional places, especially if there was a bumper crop of white oak acorns. As the years progressed, the quail increasingly moved to the woods, becoming more like their woodland cousins, the ruffed grouse.

Old-timers grumbled that it was "them damn Mexican quail" and swore that the introduction of exotic birds had corrupted the native bobwhite.

"Won't hold for dogs none, run like goddam rabbits. And they're smaller than the old bobwhite, too, by God!"

The Conservation Department had experimented with Mexican quail a half century before, but any genetic infusions had long since dissipated. What we were seeing was the result of selective breeding. The dumb fencerow-sitting bobwhites of our childhood had been shot out, and those that had escaped to the woods had survived. Give any creature a couple hundred generations to alter its genetic makeup and you'll find dramatic behavioral changes.

We learned that quail love briars, and we learned the hard way that if you want to root coveys out you have to go in after them. We learned that brush pants and chaps turn briars far better than blue jeans.

I learned that there is a stage beyond the limit of human endurance where, if the incentive is strong enough, you can force yourself a few more steps. Sometimes that extra yard was the distance to the house, where the yellow glow of the lights was a beacon and a promise, but sometimes it was a final covey flush and the decision to go after them rather than head home. We were torn. You hate to leave a covey broken at sunset; it's tough enough for the birds in winter when they're coveyed up, butt to butt, but far worse when they're separated.

Then they're vulnerable not only to the icy grip of night cold but also to nocturnal predators. Chances are, quail separated from the covey at sunset reside in something's alimentary canal by daybreak.

Usually we didn't follow them, but sometimes if we saw a few land we'd make another swing and see if we could pick off a final bird or two.

LEARNING TO quail hunt is simple: Find good quail habitat, get a decent dog, and walk around in the habitat. There are no secrets, no shortcuts. Early in the season, the birds can be almost anywhere, including in the middle of fields, where they roost to avoid raptors perching in the fencerows.

A good ice storm or a heavy snow will knock down a lot of cover and concentrate quail in the traditional places—fencerows, gullies, brushy patches. From then until season's end, quail are more predictable but also fewer in number.

On public areas, quail hunters almost all make the mistake of hunting good-looking cover, especially near parking lots. It's easy. It's also heavily hunted. Why follow your fellow hunters like pit mules, trudging one after the other?

Instead, hike to the back side of the area. Hunt old fields and woodlots. If it's hard to get to, that's where quail will go. And hunt late in the season. Quail near the boundaries of public areas fly off the area to protected private land but return later when pressure eases.

The principles are the same on private ground. Few areas escape hunting pressure, and just because a farm is private doesn't mean it isn't hunted.

The quail react the same way—they look for unpressured areas, the old fields and small woodlots where hunters don't go.

Every quail is born with a Dunkirk mentality, a built-in instinct to put water between itself and danger, like the British soldiers who fled across the English Channel to fight the Germans another day. Quail that flew across rivers survived to breed new river fliers; birds caught in the open were easy targets, and their stupid traits vanished in the genetic whirlpool.

Today, a smart hunter can bulk his bag by realizing that after the first flush of easy hunting early in the season, quail go to their last line of defense—the riverbank.

Obviously, there isn't enough territory for all quail to retreat to the river, but it is a favored location. Late in the season, coveys along a river will be larger than those out in the more open areas, because they haven't been hit as hard.

The vegetation is more rank and the shooting is often fleeting, at birds jinking through brush and trees—almost like grouse shooting. If a hunter does come close, the birds often flush wild across the river without offering a shot. They're often guarded by a dense strip of vegetation between a crop field and the riverbank trees—usually tall weeds like horseweed or a jungle of willow sprouts. But if you can fight through this stuff, you'll find a bench of fairly clear ground where the bankside trees have shaded out growth. This is where pressed quail coveys rest.

They range into the crop field to feed, but they return to the riverbank because it's a short, quick flight to safety. Unless you're back there with them, a covey will let you walk right on by. In my experience, most hunters don't send their dogs into that jungle. They want to see the dog work, so they let Ol' Sport cast the field edge. Hunting that way, Ol' Sport is going to miss the riverbank covey.

You and the dog both need to be where the quail are, not where you think they should be. A beeper collar is almost imperative, because you won't see much of the dog but you can hear the point signal.

The relatively open area between the vegetation belt and the river is often a resting place for woodcock, a bonus bird for the quail hunter (or perhaps quail are a bonus bird for woodcock hunters).

Once I got into a lowland pole thicket alongside a cornstubble field that had been hunted and, predictably, held no quail. But the thicket was full of woodcock. I shot a couple, then decided to cross the creek into a jungle of cedars, broom sedge, and brush. There was a huge covey of quail just across the creek that no one else had worked hard enough to find.

The ideal way to hunt the vegetation belt between the field and the river is with one hunter inside, one out. Often a covey will flush into the weeds or straight ahead, and it's really tough shooting for the inside man, which is why you should alternate dirty duty.

But some of those birds will loft above the towering weeds, giving the outside shooter a quick but open shot. Since so many shot birds fall where they're unfindable without a dog, it's imperative to have a good dead-bird dog along.

If you cut between river quail and the river, the birds still will curve back toward the river, but some almost always will stop short of flying across. But if you flush them directly at the river, every single one will fly it, every time without fail.

Once I hunted along Missouri's Moreau River on a chilly, late-season afternoon. A covey that I'd molested periodically (without much effect) flushed wild ahead of me, and I watched them cross the river and filter into the tree-shrouded bluff there. I knew exactly where those birds had gone, in contrast to most quail flushes today, when you're lucky to find any scatters.

The problem was, the nearest crossing was a mile away—unless I waded the river. But I'd had enough of that devilish covey, so I stripped off my boots and britches, gritted my teeth, and waded in. The frigid water was numbing and the gravel bit at my tender feet, but then I was across. The dogs swam over, looking sideways at me as if expecting further and perhaps more dangerous weirdness. I got my clothes back on and clambered up the steep slope to the bluff top, an old field.

A point. Two birds burst out of the thick grass and I killed one. Then the second dog went down a few yards farther on. I dumped that bird, too. It was shooting out of old sporting books, in the open, with birds as tight as a brother-in-law's wallet.

Before I ran out the string I'd killed three birds and missed two. It was enough, and I hiked to the normal crossing and splashed back to my original side of the river. I got more birds from that covey in one ten-minute shoot than I'd gotten in the previous two months, just because I was willing to sacrifice my body a bit.

If the river is small enough, you can hunt both sides and really catch birds in a nutcracker. For years we hunted the Mussel Fork, a north Missouri stream about ten to fifteen feet wide but too deep to wade. We'd start at a county highway, usually with a couple of hunters on each side, and work it for a mile or so through the farm where we had permission to hunt.

Invariably we'd move a couple of coveys, and invariably they'd fly back and forth across the stream, giving shots to both parties.

If you're hunting that way, you must keep pace with the other hunters so you don't flush birds ahead or behind them. And you must be wary of shots across the stream so you don't sprinkle a buddy.

If the stream has crossings, you're set, but they're often hard to find. I *have* crossed on logs, but I'm no Wallenda, and a couple of times I've come close to doing a foward one-and-a-half into icy water. That's no fun if you're a couple of miles from the car and it's nineteen degrees.

The safest way to cross on a log is by scooting on your butt, but that's only relative safety. Common sense says if you can't wade it or jump across, forget the river quail and find some new birds.

Common sense is a commodity bird dogs completely lack. They'll go onto thin ice after downed birds, and that's a good way to lose a cherished dog. It has happened. No quail is worth that heartache. Make sure you can control your dog if you shoot birds over ice or icy water.

On the other hand, there are times when common sense deserts the hunter and enters the dog. It happened to me in the 1991–92 season. A whole new world opened for one of my dogs.

This river covey represented all that's tough in quail hunting. I'd walked an entire crop-field bottom, using all my tricks, without moving a bird.

There was one possibility, a small field that lay like a peninsula between the river and a slough. There's only one way to cross onto the old field, a tiptoe across logs jumbled in a muddy swale. Slip off and you're knee-deep in muck. The field is small and choked with weeds, some eight or ten feet tall. It's unpromising at best.

But it also held a covey, hiding out from me and the other hunters who'd trudged the bottom. When Dacques, the French Brittany, locked down, I knew the birds, only a couple dozen feet from the riverbank, would fly the river. Nothing I could do about it.

Sure enough, they flushed straight across. I killed the first, missed the second, and I knew the dead bird had landed in the river.

There it was, floating peacefully downstream near the far bank—too far to reach with a stick. The dogs didn't see it, and I watched in frustration as it drifted away. There were no shallows as far as I could see.

I kept pace for a couple hundred yards then stopped to ponder. Dacques waded into the stream, and I realized the muddy water wasn't very deep after all. Maybe I could wade out and intercept the approaching bird.

I stripped, except for a tee shirt (modesty, after all, is a virtue), and waded thigh-deep into the numbing water, but the bird still was out of reach and I wasn't willing to swim for it.

Dacques stood beside me, puzzled. I grabbed a stick and pitched it close to the bird. Dacques spotted the quail and his eyes widened. *A quail!* he thought. *Where in the hell did that come from?*

He swam out and retrieved it, and as I was putting my clothes back on, I glanced down at the river.

There was Dacques, belly-deep in the river, looking expectantly upstream.

Waiting for the next quail.

SMART HUNTERS mark maps of their favorite places with covey locations, because a covey will be close to the mark every year, given stable habitat conditions.

Such maps let a hunter high-grade his hunting day, especially in lean years. Why spend six hours prospecting when you can hit-and-run covey locations from previous years?

A few years back I hunted several small public wildlife areas within a few miles of each other. Three were river accesses, the other a sizable area.

The first one is about thirty acres. There was one small managed field, plus some old field going to sprouts and a thick sprout jungle that often held woodcock. I'd run the sprout jungle during the brief time when woodcock and quail season overlapped, then work the fringe of the food plot and through the old field.

The hunt took about thirty minutes. I'd often come out with a quail or two—the resident covey would fly the river, but I would take a bird just about each time I flushed them. Since no one else was hunting the covey, I'd trim it by four or five birds in the season.

Once, I killed two birds with one shot when they crossed just as I shot. Another time I killed a limit of woodcock while my wife watched, the only time she's ever gone bird hunting with me.

Next, I'd cut cross-country to the second access, which was somewhat larger and also rarely hunted. This area is about 150 acres and regularly carried three coveys of quail. I could count on moving one or two just about every hunt and occasionally would bump all three. One escaped into the woods, another flew the river, and the third would scatter through the interior of the area—the most vulnerable of the three, but even then never shot out.

That was an hour hunt.

Then I'd take gravel roads to the third area, also about 150 acres, but much of it in fescue. This area had a long ditch along a wet-weather creek that intersected a second drainage, which then flowed into the Osage River.

A covey invariably rested somewhere along that ditch. Sometimes I'd put up a second covey on the back side of the area that would fly into the wooded river bluffs.

This hunt also took about an hour. So in a half day's hunt, I would have the potential of six known coveys. That's not bad anywhere. And most of those coveys were not hunted by anyone but me.

And I still had the afternoon to hunt an eight-hundred-acre wildlife area that at one time held at least eight coveys I knew about, probably more I didn't.

Hunting hasn't been that good since the Conservation Department, in its infatuation with "ecosystem management," decided to abandon management of small areas and let them grow up in sprouts.

Habitat changes, and so does quail hunting. Wouldn't it be nice, though, if it occasionally changed for the better?

Most states have maps of public areas; some have atlases or other comprehensive map and information publications. Contact your state wildlife agency. An invaluable reference is the National Wildlife Federation's annual Conservation Directory, which lists addresses, phone numbers, and contact names for all state agencies and other government and private entities.

To order, call 800-432-6564. The price has been $25 recently ($20 for NWF members).

# 4

# WHERE AND WHAT?

THE BOBWHITE QUAIL is the least imposing of the North American quails, but by far the most widely distributed and hunted. As I've mentioned, an estimated 35 million bobwhites fall to hunters' guns each season, compared with 7 to 8 million of the other hunted species combined. A cock bobwhite, with his white head markings, is an attractive bird, but stand him next to a mountain quail with its long, two-feathered crest and the bobwhite looks positively dowdy—a country rube compared to an uptown dandy.

All the other quails are more flamboyant than the bobwhite. There are some thirty-six quail species in the New World, including such oddities as the tree quail (bearded, long-tailed, and buffy-crowned) and the singing quail.

No hunter will see those birds in the wilds of the United States. We have six species of quail here: bobwhite, Mearns', mountain, Gambel's, scaled, and California, or valley, quail. Some consider the rare masked bobwhite a seventh species, though most think it is a subspecies. Taxonomists have been arguing over quail species for decades. Part of the problem is that quail hybridize readily, creating what appears to be another species.

Some western states have outstanding quail hunting, especially Arizona and California (where the bird named for the state is the most prevalent of several species). California quail also are, next to bobwhites, the most widely distributed of the quails; they're found in five states and British Columbia. Scaled, or blue, quail also are in five states, but no Canadian provinces. Texas has the top population of scaled quail. Gambel's quail also inhabit eight states, with Arizona the hot spot.

Western quail are lightly tapped and widely dispersed compared to their eastern cousin. Bobwhite quail occur in nearly forty states and Ontario. The best populations are in my home, Missouri, along with Texas, Oklahoma, Kansas, and Georgia. Tennessee and Kentucky have good quail hunting, along with southern Iowa in good years and Illinois where there is decent habitat. Most southeastern states, once great for bobwhite quail, have declined seriously because of habitat loss.

Each year I do a quail and pheasant survey for *Gun Dog* magazine, where I've written a conservation column for many years. And each year the story from the Southeast is increasingly grim.

The universal complaint from upland wildlife biologists in the Carolinas, Virginia, Alabama, Mississippi, and Louisiana is loss of habitat. Much of Georgia's kill is on plantations managed for quail. The rest of the state suffers from the habitat malaise that plagues the rest of the Southeast. Further, the Conservation Reserve Program, which has been a godsend to pheasants in many states, has not proved as much of a boon to quail.

Much of the 37 million CRP acres went to grass, often fescue, an abomination for wildlife. In the Southeastern states, much

CRP acreage is in pine trees, equally useless for quail. CRP was favorable only in the first couple of years of the ten-year set-aside contracts, when the idled ground grew up in annual weeds that provided food as well as cover. After that, grass took over.

If I were to choose a spot to quail hunt, year after year, it would be the Flint Hills of Kansas. Eastern Kansas seems to hold a better population of quail over the long haul than any place I've hunted.

And the Flint Hills, an irregular area from Topeka west to Salina, from north of Manhattan to south of Winfield, is a wonderful ecosystem that offers both good quail hunting and great scenery. Kansas hunters regularly take more than 2 million quail.

The best hunting in Texas is north-central and far south, not the eastern part of the state where it borders Louisiana. In boom years, nothing can touch Texas quail hunting. Twenty coveys a day is not unusual, and I've heard stories about rousting fifty coveys in south Texas.

That abundance is inconceivable to me. In Missouri, a dozen-covey day is something to remember forever. But Texas hunting can bust, too, and when it does, the hunting is as poor as poor hunting anywhere else.

Oklahoma may have the most stable and best overall quail hunting in the country. In fact, Oklahoma is the only state to report no long-term decline in quail abundance over the past thirty years. Sooner hunters kill an estimated 3 million quail almost every season, the best in the country (in 1992 it was a whopping 3.4 million).

That tops Texas's good-year estimate of perhaps 2 million, but Texas quail are underhunted because of access problems. Missouri hunters will kill 1.5 million birds in a good year, the same as Tennessee.

Alabama hunters kill about 400,000 quail a year, but the trend is down because of habitat loss. Florida hunters take about 300,000 birds, similar to the kill in the Carolinas. The Virginia bag is about 200,000. Mississippi and Louisiana report low kills—Mississippi 200,000 and declining, Louisiana 100,000 in a good year.

Mississippi is the prime example of what has happened to southern quail hunting. In 1980, Mississippi hunters took an estimated 1.5 million quail.

Statistics are indicators only, but quail researchers are coming up with better than the educated guesses they made for half a century, thanks to radio-tagged birds that can't hide from a receiver.

The radio collar is the Rosetta Stone of quail research. Accurate quail studies waited on electronic miniaturization, which only happened in the past few years. Now a quail fitted with a tiny transmitter (about the size of a quarter and weighing less) drags around its electronic leash, and a researcher with a receiver can find the bird every time.

I've been fascinated by these transmitters since they appeared. One or two quail in a covey spy on the entire group, letting biologists know where the birds are at any given moment and what's happening to them.

Think of the potential: Researchers are finding out just how good bird dogs are at finding available birds (no more than 50 percent on average), where quail roost, where they spend their days, what they do in bad weather (or good weather, for that matter), survival (both during the hunting season and during the rest of the year), what they're eating (by inference from where they are), and a host of other life-history items that no one could be sure of before.

Many long-held beliefs about quail have been knocked askew or discredited. It's not just birds with failed nests that renest, for example. Quail often bring off a second successful brood and even a third, if the weather is good.

Quail survival from season to season is probably less than originally thought. Biologists used to think perhaps 10 to 20 percent would survive a year, but the figure, according to one study, is about five percent.

Except in foul weather, quail roost in fields with good overhead cover (weeds or grass or something about knee-high). Quail seem to have a built-in aversion to exposing themselves, probably because of threats from avian predators. A covey doesn't want to cross bare ground to get to a food plot, so if you're planting food plots, put them next to good escape cover.

"WHIR-R-R—UP they got all at once! what a jostle—what a hub-bub! Bang! bang! crack! bang! Four barrels exploded in an instant, almost simultaneously; and two sharp, unmeaning cracks announced that, by some means or other, Frank Forester's gun had missed fire with both barrels."

Forester (actually an English expatriate named Henry Herbert) came to the United States in 1849 and was a pioneer outdoor writer. He was talking about a hunt in southern New York State, not far from the U.S. Military Academy at West Point. Wild quail in any numbers in New York State are long gone.

Bobwhite quail have been a shrinking resource for decades. Areas that once held quail have been vacant for many years. My mother was from northwest Wisconsin, and old-timers there can remember when there were quail.

The national statistical summary of quail populations shows a depressing series of minus signs. Overall, the continental population has declined at more than 2 percent per year since the 1960s. It doesn't take a mathematical genius to figure that quail hunting is not what it once was.

Further, the decline is the most drastic in bobwhite range. Western quail populations are relatively stable. Why? Habitat loss is the universal culprit, and at least so far, the West has been losing habitat less drastically than the East and South.

Until the end of World War Two, farmers plowed with horses or small, inefficient tractors. But the postwar years brought improved machinery and new pesticides and herbicides that allowed bigger fields, more intensive agriculture—and the consequent loss of the old brushy fields, fencerows, and gullies. Bye-bye Bob White.

Even crops changed. In Missouri, more than 90 percent of the state's pasture and hay fields once were legumes—alfalfa and clover especially, which provided greens and seeds for quail. Now more than 95 percent of those same fields are in fescue, an utterly useless grass for quail.

What's the answer for us poor bird hunters? We don't all live on the land where we hunt. Nor can we afford to lease the increasingly rare good bird habitat. Nor do we all know someone who has access to good bird hunting.

All wildlife managers face a common dilemma: Do you provide a *quality* experience or just an experience? In other words, do you regulate hunters so those that do get to hunt will find game (or fish in the case of trophy regulations)? Or do you apply a one-regulation-fits-all format, knowing that most hunters or anglers won't score very well?

From a hunter's standpoint, it's equally frustrating. The quail hunter wants to exercise himself and his dogs but also wants to see quail. It's depressing to walk all day and see no birds, or perhaps only a small covey that flushes wild into the woods, but it's common where there is heavy hunting pressure.

On the other hand, luck-of-the-draw hunts, where hunting is regulated, also are frustrating. You may not be drawn. You may not be available to hunt when you are drawn. You may not be able to hunt where you'd like or as long as you'd like. You're restricted.

I never liked hunting public areas for ducks because you're almost always confined to the blind you drew. It drives you crazy to be stuck in a sterile blind and see ducks dropping into a set not far away.

Hunters, being free spirits and explorers by nature, resent being confined by regulation.

There are many ways to regulate quail hunting: half-day or alternate-day hunts, hunter numbers controlled by draw or application, area zoning, restricted bag limits, short seasons—probably more. Such regulations are common in waterfowl hunting but fairly new for quail hunters, at least where I live. And they apply only to public land; private-land hunters still have the advantage of hunting under statewide regulations.

The caveat is that good private-land quail hunting is shrinking every year. Public land, no matter how well managed for quail, can't provide enough territory for all the hunters who want to use it. Areas aren't big enough, and public agencies don't have the money to buy enough land and manage it for quail.

Further, there are powerful competing interests on public land. There are more deer hunters than quail hunters and, most places, as many turkey hunters as quail hunters. Those species take somewhat different management. If wildlife agencies listen to the hunters with the most clout, quail inevitably get the short end of the stick. There simply is more wildlife revenue in deer, if not in turkeys.

And, depressingly, deer take less money to manage than quail do. Let an area grow up in brush, with a few food plots scattered around, and you have pretty fair deer habitat but lousy quail habitat. Quail need edge, the division between one habitat type and another.

Strip cropping, small fields of a variety of foods good for quail, mixtures of woody cover interspersed with seed crops—these are all necessary to maximize the quail potential but not to top out the deer herd. So it isn't surprising that wildlife agencies with limited budgets are reluctant to spend what's necessary to keep quail in peak condition.

By continuing poor land stewardship, farmers don't help. Every time I criticize poor farming the entire agricultural community jumps on me, even the good land stewards. As a group, farmers are quick to sense insult and take offense. While they might criticize a neighbor's poor farming among themselves, they don't like outsiders doing it.

Yet the agricultural community is rife with land abuse. The fall of 1989 was dry—the driest November on record in Missouri—and birds, dogs, and bird hunters all suffered.

This continued a string of drought years that made the 1980s nearly as damaging as the 1930s. We learned hard lessons sixty years ago. Farms blew away and fortunes with them. Dust Bowl dust shrouded the Capitol in Washington as lawmakers wrestled with the Depression.

As a result of the Dirty Thirties, farmers planted windbreaks of Osage orange, learned dryland farming, and tried to live within the sometimes limited offerings of nature—for about a decade.

For the past fifty years we've been trying to forget our hard-won lessons. By the 1980s, Missouri was second nationally in soil erosion. The 1989 fall was dry, hot, and generally windy. So what did farmers do? Why they fall-plowed, of course.

They exposed their fragile topsoil to wind erosion. Field after field turned brown. They ignored fifty years of information and education about soil erosion. "If I had my way, I'd take the tractor keys of every Missouri farmer in November and issue him a bird dog," said one disgusted soil conservationist. "They've got equipment and they've got time on their hands and that's a dangerous combination." The farmer who lives for today's crop and lets the farm blow or wash away is selling his children's birthright, and that is a shameful thing.

The major loss is to the soil base that feeds us all, but from a more narrow viewpoint, we bird hunters lose our sport. The birds lose habitat and food, and that results in fewer birds. I drove past countless fields with no ring of cover and with bare dirt from bare fencewire to bare fencewire. There was a shrubby gully, but it was bordered on both sides by fields gone belly-up to the plow.

I hunted with a young farmer, an outdoor type who believes he is a conservationist. Yet he scoffed at the local Soil Conservation Service district conservationist as a bureaucrat who likes to use big words. He made light of the conservation plans required on all farms if they are to receive federal aid and said he didn't need their money anyway. He had fall-plowed almost every field because, as he told me, he and his father have more than two dozen vehicles, ranging from pickup trucks to huge combines, and they don't like to see them sitting there. "I plowed this field up for the first time," he said. "Wanted to see if it would grow anything."

They are big-time operators, true proponents of the philosophy that bigger is better, that there is a technological solution for every problem. Americans have always found another rich valley to spoil over the next ridge, so why worry about ruining this valley? The frontier mentality should have died a long time ago, but it lives on—except that we've run out of valleys.

In time we'll be forced to face up to our problems, probably by dealing with a sudden crisis, because that's the way we operate. We'll find that chemicals won't prop up the soil anymore and are bad for us. Chemical fertilizers don't replace trace elements, and pesticides kill organisms essential for good soil health, and probably also for ours.

None of the young landowner's actions are done out of malice. He, like most landowners, has an affection for wildlife. He thinks he's doing as much as he can afford to do for the wildlife on his farms—although he did manage to slip in the comment that deer are a real pest and eat a huge amount of crops.

He suffers from the common landowner attitude that considers wildlife a by-product of the farm, not a product. There is a subconscious discounting of anything gotten free from the land. I know a farmer who loves blackberry cobbler, yet he brush-hogged all the wild blackberry canes from his farm and then bought some from a nursery.

By considering wildlife a by-product the farmer diminishes it. He invests nothing in it, therefore it is worth nothing. Aesthetic value really is of no value to those who think practically. The sight of the covey or the buck in the back pasture is only vaguely gratifying, but it is not money in the bank, and when push comes to shove the critters get shoved.

The Missouri farmer who complains about the deer could shoot at least four to supplement his food supply, a substantial chunk of meat—the equivalent of at least six hundred dollars at the grocery store. He'll tell you he doesn't have time to hunt deer. He does have time, though, to plow up his wildlife food and cover when he could be supplementing his food supply.

He (and by "he" I mean those who do what the young farmer does) resists change. He can take enormous risks financially—hundreds of thousands of dollars, even millions—but he's unwilling to change his farming methods to save his soil, to diversify his land use, or to raise more on the land than cash crops.

The confirmed monocrop farmer isn't likely to change, even change to another money-making system. I know a landowner whose lessee planted sunflowers, a good cash crop in many places. "I spent my whole life trying to kill those damn weeds and he's planting them," the landowner said in disgust. He understood corn and beans. Sunflowers were as unwelcome as Johnsongrass. How do you convert people like that to conservation farming? How do you turn them from intensive land use to a system that favors crop rotation, reduced emphasis on chemicals, even a tolerance for wildlife habitat in the fencerows and field edges?

Where you list problems, you try to find solutions. The Conservation Reserve Program is a stopgap. It is a federal program in which highly erodible land is leased for ten years and must be planted to a cover crop. The goal is 44 million acres nationally. By 1995, 37 million acres were enrolled. Farmers are being paid to do what they should do out of concern for the earth they live on, but not to quibble.

But even CRP has its limitations. In some cases the cover crop is worthless for wildlife—fescue, for example. And gradually, even the best CRP land will become grassland, which is marginal for upland wildlife. We have perhaps three to five years of excellent bird hunting on the CRP acres, then a declining resource for the remaining life of the program.

And if CRP goes the way of the lamented Soil Bank Program of the 1950s, the acres protected today from erosion will be plowed up for some wonder crop of the next century, probably fence to fence.

Maybe the painful answer is leased hunting. Give a farmer dollars to keep habitat on the land and he will. Of course, leasing puts hunting in the hands of the moneyed few and disenfranchises those without the money or contacts to nail down good leases. That is indeed a painful solution.

IF QUAIL IN southern states face the problem of habitat loss, at least they normally don't have the problem of winter survival. But in the northern part of the bobwhite's range a severe winter can hammer quail hard, and the aftereffects will take several years to get over.

In 1983 there was a severe snow and ice storm in Missouri coupled with a long period of extreme cold. Quail froze in their roosts and some areas of the state became almost quail-free. The storm and record low temperatures knocked quail back for the next two seasons, and only several mild winters with good carry over of birds (coupled with the advent of the Conservation Reserve Program) let populations rebound.

Researchers started looking for answers to the problems of winter survival. The Missouri Conservation Department devised an "artificial storm," creating under laboratory conditions what quail face: temperatures from forty-one degrees down to zero, with varied wind speeds and different combinations of bird numbers—twelve, representing a full covey; six, representing a shotback covey; and one, representing a bird separated from the covey, perhaps by a late-afternoon flush.

At the same time, researchers followed radio-tagged birds through the winter. Do winter-stressed quail suffer a loss of productivity the next breeding season, either in the number of eggs laid or in fewer surviving young? Is nesting delayed while they recoup body condition lost in winter?

"Below a certain temperature, quail have to burn calories just to maintain body temperature," said Wes Burger, the biologist who ran the study. "The more energy they burn, the more food they have to eat and probably the poorer body condition they're going to be in."

The laboratory winter was produced in an airtight chamber, where the researchers could control both wind speed and temperature. "We assume that because quail roost in coveys in the wintertime there's some adaptive benefit to it—a thermal advantage because there is less body surface exposed. The more they're up against another bird, the warmer they're going to be," he said.

The artificial winter had advantages—Burger could do in two hours what would take two months in the field. "We let the birds acclimate for the first hour, then take repeated measurements of the oxygen consumption the second hour," he said. "The chamber is airtight, so we know the oxygen going into the chamber and what comes out."

Birds were exposed to four temperatures: between thirty-five and forty degrees, which is the point at which quail must start burning fat to maintain body heat; freezing; fifteen degrees; and zero. Wind speeds varied from none to six miles per hour and twelve miles per hour.

To measure body condition, Burger used an electromagnetic scanner, which feeds ultrasound readings through a computer to measure body fat, protein content, water content, and other physiological information, all without harming the bird. Thus a live bird can be exposed to different conditions, scanned, and made to tell how the conditions are affecting it without suffering the fate of a quail in the wild: death.

Before the various experiments were finished, the researchers had radio-equipped more than a thousand quail. Now that the study is ended, quail managers have, for the first time, hard evidence of what quail both want and need to make it through the winter.

They found that quail choose night roosts that provide the best compromise between insulation against heat loss (quail body temperature is a torrid 107 degrees, and they begin to burn calories when the air temperature drops below 75.4 degrees) and protection from predators.

Quail roost tail-to-tail in a circle, and this tight covey knot does two things: It gives the birds communal warmth and protection from predators—if they flush, they confuse a predator with their multidirectional explosion.

Quail almost always roost well out in grassy or weedy fields, unless snow or ice knocks the cover down and forces them to woody draws or other woody cover. The fields are a compromise; they'd be warmer in heavy woody cover but more vulnerable to predators (raptors hunting from trees or ground predators traveling a fencerow or brushy draw, for example).

Somehow, quail have learned to choose a finely balanced compromise—instinct that almost looks like thought. "The dumb ones are dead," says Tom Dailey, a quail research biologist for the Missouri Conservation Department.

Roosts where there are many seed-bearing plants also save a quail's energy. They're sleeping at the dinner table. "They don't fly anywhere from the roost," Burger says. "They just start walking and eating."

The study was not easy because there are so many factors involved. "It's a complex problem," explains Burger. "Weather itself is complex. It isn't just cold alone, but wind, which brings about the well-known windchill effect. Then there's ice, snow, and rain. We talk about managing quail, but what we're really managing is habitat for quail."

Quail managers now have a formula for habitat (type of plants, height, spacing, and so forth), which they can apply to public land and can recommend for private land.

The miniature radio transmitters that have aided quail researchers were developed in 1981 by biologists Brad Mueller, Lorvel Shields, and Robert Darling at Florida's famed Tall Timbers private research center.

They knew a quail seldom travels more than a half mile from where it is trapped, so they figured a transmitter with a range of half a kilometer (biologists traffic in the metric system) would be efficient. They also knew the transmitter would have to last a minimum of ninety days, since quail are tough to catch in the summer.

They found that quail wearing backpack-type transmitters are visible and become easy prey for hawks, so they decided to go with a chest-mounted transmitter. The battery is coin-shaped, about the size of a quarter, and it weighs five to seven grams (roughly a quarter ounce). This is equivalent to a two-hundred-pound man carrying a six-pound load—not a crippling burden.

The researchers say the coin-shaped battery is biologically important because of its low profile. I can testify to that. A friend shot a quail carrying a transmitter. We didn't realize the bird was wired because the battery had nestled among the bird's breast feathers. My buddy happened to feel the battery as he was putting the quail in his shell vest.

"We have frequently captured birds and been unable to tell if they were instrumented until they were in hand," the researchers say. "There are advantages other than low visibility," Mueller says. "We have measured crop-content weights as high as fifteen grams, more than double the average weight of our transmitters. It seems reasonable to consider quail 'preadapted' to carrying weight in this body location."

In a study in northern Missouri, carried out partly on CRP land, partly on private farmland, Wes Burger found that the preferred night roost is on the ground in a field of annual weeds that aren't too thick, at an average of seventy-five meters from the nearest woody vegetation. Quail usually use woods, brush piles, and sumac thickets as night roosts only when they're forced to by bad weather. They regularly use woody areas during the daytime. "It's important for them to have vertical protection around them," Burger says. "Standing weeds can cut wind speed a hundred percent. We found roosting quail at twenty-four below doing just fine."

Quail on the CRP land had a slightly higher winter survival rate than those on the farmed land. "The farmland birds may have had more so-called hot food—high-quality corn and milo," Burger says. "But they had to burn more energy to get it because the cover wasn't as protective. The more energy quail burn, the more food they have to eat and probably the poorer body condition they're going to be in." This may create problems in nesting.

Quail are tenacious nesters. From 75 to 95 percent of hens that live to the end of nesting season will bring off a brood. "We know of hens that have nested three times in a summer, and they could have had two or three other nests that we didn't know about," Burger says.

Quail nests face two major problems. Predators are the greatest by far. Skunks, opossums, raccoons, foxes, coyotes, snakes, and housecats all find and destroy nests, and some destroy the hen as well.

The other problem is human activity, especially mowing—not only of hayfields but also of roadside ditches, which are a favored quail-nesting area.

The radio transmitters have documented something that quail biologist Jack Stanford theorized years ago: Quail can have two broods in a season.

"There are two ways a hen will double-clutch," Burger says. "One is by raising a brood to an age where it can fend for itself, then renesting; the other is to lay a clutch of eggs for the male to incubate, then lay another clutch for herself."

Researchers know that about 25 percent of quail nests are incubated by males. Sometimes it's because the female was killed and the male took over, but other times it's because the female is busy with another nest.

"The missing piece to the puzzle is that we didn't have the chicks radio-tagged," Burger says. "So we don't know what's happening to them." Chicks are extremely vulnerable to chilling for their first fifteen days. Then they need high-protein food to help develop feathers for protection.

"If a chick can make it to six weeks old, he has a pretty good chance of doing all right. Although quail don't have a very good chance at any age."

A longtime biologist once said, "The first step in managing something is to find out how it works." That's where quail researchers are after decades of educated guessing.

So radio transmitters and other techniques are telling researchers what quail need. But the needing and the getting are two different things. The line below the bottom line is, How do you get landowners to do what's right for quail?

So far, there aren't any electromagnetic scanners to accomplish that magic.

# 5

# IT TAKES A DOG

THERE ARE THREE factors in quail hunting: hunter, dog, and bird. Certainly you can quail hunt without a dog, but it's no longer really quail hunting. It's like Mark Twain's definition of golf: "A good walk spoiled."

Puppies are the raw material from which the finished dog is fashioned. Some hunters prefer to buy finished or started dogs. To me, that's like calling wild turkeys with a record player or paying someone to take Raquel Welch to dinner while you sit across the restaurant and eat a hot dog and watch. Puppies make you young, and in turn puppies become what you make them.

Even the most talented surgeon can't graft a good nose onto the end of a puppy's muzzle, but given good bloodlines, the little guy should have the nose and bird desire the breed is notable for and the brain to go with it. All the rest is a blank blackboard waiting for your deft touch.

You can buy a puppy or raise your own. If a puppy is yours from conception on, you control not only his creation but also every development of his life. It's a godlike feeling. But raising puppies is somewhat like raising a garden. Unless you're really equipped for it, it's a lot of trouble, unbelievably time-consuming, and may well cost more than buying a puppy from a breeder.

But buying a puppy isn't foolproof. I once helped a friend pick a puppy from a kennel where there were too many dogs living in poor conditions—dirt runs and cramped housing. The kennel owner wasn't insensitive to the dogs' needs, but his puppies simply weren't given exceptional care. Aside from the unsanitary facilities, the dogs were not "socialized." That's an animal behaviorist's term for fooling around with a puppy—playing with it. When you raise a puppy, you'll play with it. You bond with the pup until it considers you mom, God, and the American flag all rolled into one. It will do anything to please you.

A puppy that hasn't had intensive human contact, especially with its master-to-be, tends to be uncertain and timid. We made that mistake with three puppies from our last litter.

They didn't sell right away, and I was hunting the older dogs and just didn't have time to work with the puppies, especially one-on-one. They also were treated as chew toys by their older cousin and gradually they withdrew to one another, timid around humans. They acted as if I were going to beat them even though I'd never been rough on them at all.

I feel bad about it because their poor development is a direct result of my indifference. Perhaps they'll come out of it and become both bird dogs and delightful friends. All our other dogs have—but the other dogs have had the advantage of early contact and a great deal of fussing over.

If you get a puppy, *live* with it. You simply can't spoil a puppy with attention. Of course there is a time to be firm and establish who's boss, but anyone who says treating a bird dog as a pet will ruin it is full of bull.

Many breeders don't have time for socialization, and if you get a dog that's much older than seven weeks from an impersonal kennel, you'll have a tougher time making that dog an extension of you.

SHOULD YOU LOOK to line breeding or mixed bloodlines? Line breeding, in common with its human equivalent, inbreeding, can produce geniuses or idiots; if you're lucky, you'll buy a genius dog. But it's fairly easy to make a mistake picking a seven-week-old puppy. Unless you have a sharp eye, you can miss the idiot child at that age and wind up with a dud for the next dozen years. Better to take a pup from parents of different families, different bloodlines.

I know about two pups produced by a very famous setter line breeder. One I never saw, but the owner still trembles with anger when he talks about the dog. "The son of a bitch was retarded!" he growls. "It never learned anything in two years. I swear if you stuck its nose right in a covey of quail it wouldn't know what you were trying to do."

He finally got rid of the dog. The other pup was one I hunted behind for woodcock—way behind. I saw the dog briefly as we got out of the car and again when it was time to leave. Actually, I occasionally saw it as we threaded through a dense bottom of sprouts. You can tell when a dog is hunting, and this dog was not hunting. Skylarking is as close as I can get to describing it, but that implies an attraction to a species of bird. This dolt wasn't attracted to any species of birds that I could tell.

It did pose beautifully for photos, however, which is something the line is famous for. Part of the problem was a lack of discipline—the owner had no control over the dog—but I think most of the problem was genetic deficiency.

Before you acquire a bird dog, read two references. One is *Gun Dog Breeds*, by Charles Fergus (Lyons & Burford, 1992), a fine roundup of available hunting dog breeds, with their strengths and weaknesses and sources of more information about each.

The other reference is *The Intelligence of Dogs*, by Stanley Coren (Macmillan, 1994). This is a wonderful insight into the way dogs think (and, yes, dogs *do* think—sometimes in surprisingly sophisticated ways).

These books will help you pick a puppy and understand its thought processes. Other books on training (I am a fan of the late Richard Wolters's landmark book *Gun Dog*) will tell you how to translate your understanding into action.

MY DOG BREEDING has been of the hobby variety. My wife and I had children with far less discussion than we gave to breeding our female dogs.

Before our first experiment, I had still fresh in my mind the hot ovulatory odyssey of a friend who finished with a $2,800 puppy that had only half a tail.

To protect both the guilty and the innocent I will not name names, but if you are the owner of a bitch and are ever tempted to breed her, remember this story and don't say you weren't warned.

My friend had a nice pointer bitch who came of age. She and her husband discussed transporting the bitch to a nationally famous male, a winner of top field trials. Her veterinarian (who, it might be said, had nothing to lose and, as it turned out, a whole lot to gain) urged the lady and her husband to go for it.

The going was a two-thousand-mile round-trip to Georgia. The vet took vaginal smears, which are a fairly reliable indicator of the bitch's ripening conditon—but not always, including this time.

Dogs don't really seem to enjoy procreation. I've watched slugs mate on public television, and they enjoy a languorous, positively lascivious courtship. The frantic, often painful encounter between a pair of horny dogs seems more like scratching an intolerable itch.

When the couple arrived at the kennel, their female was outraged at the indecent proposal. She snarled and snapped at the lusting male; it took two men to hold her while the stud had his way with her. "It was a rape," my friend reports.

It was also unsuccessful. The breeder allowed only one mating, with no guarantee of a pup. The couple had expected a second tryst as insurance. Nothing was in writing except the five-hundred-dollar check for the stud fee.

So far the investment included the stud fee, motel and travel, plus a novelette-sized sheaf of vet bills. The worst was yet to come. When the female failed to conceive, the owner of the stud agreed to provide nine drops of frozen semen at no charge, except for shipping. The tiny pipette of semen came in a container the size of a fraternity party beer keg. Shipping bill, seventy-five dollars.

Frozen semen can only be implanted surgically, and the surgery is tricky and major. It took four hours, and the bill for that was commensurate with the delicate nature of the operation.

This time the bitch was pregnant, but it came during what would have been her first full hunting season, so the couple lost her services in the field. And she produced only one pup, which had to be taken by cesarean section—basically a repeat of the operation that had put him there in the first place.

Understandably, the groggy bitch blamed everything on the tiny stranger at her bosom and tried to kill it. For the next nine nights, the wife of the couple dosed the mother with tranquilizers to send her into dreamland so the puppy could be plugged into mother's milk.

During the day, while the wife struggled to earn enough to pay the bills, the pup and bitch went to the vet's for in-house care. On the tenth day the bitch finally accepted her son—but somewhere in the first week she had bitten his tail, which became infected. About 25 percent of it fell off, leaving the couple with a pointer that looked as if it were aspiring to be a Brittany.

Adding insult to injury, while the couple was gone on the breeding odyssey, a neighborhood mutt bred their stay-at-home dog through the fence. The couple no longer is married, which may or may not be a result of their dog-breeding disaster. Surely it didn't help.

TRADITIONALLY, the bitch is brought to the male. Though that seems like a bit of chauvinistic animal husbandry, there is logic behind it.

Presumably, the owner of the bitch will sell the puppies and realize great revenue, while the dog owner gains only pick of the litter or a stud fee—relatively small potatoes. Those who reason this way also frequent Las Vegas crap tables expecting to earn the price of a yacht.

An alternative to chauffeuring the bitch by automobile, as we did with ours, is to ship her by air. Dave Follansbee, a pioneer breeder of French Brittanies, has wide exerience with shipping bitches and can tell more horror stories than Stephen King.

"I'm prematurely gray, a broken man," he once told me. "All of this has been too much, but I'm unable to shake loose of it."

These days dogs rarely die because of errors in air shipping, but just about anything else is possible. (In 1994, twenty puppies did die because of errors by Delta Airlines, which has one of the best reputations in dog shipping.)

Follansbee once arranged to import a French dog for a friend who lived in Boston. He and the Bostonian converged on Kennedy Airport only to find that Air France simply had forgotten to put the dog on the plane. You can scream in rage all you want, but at three thousand miles those responsible aren't going to hear it.

"You have to make up for the fact that airlines are staffed wih overworked simpletons," Follansbee said. "You have to plan every-thing."

Shipping a bitch too early in the heat period is chancy. "Don't ship until the ninth or tenth day," Follansbee says. "The psy-chological discombobulation of shipping may cause the heat to shut down. She'll go into heat again, but when?"

Follansbee once received an air-shipped bitch who promptly went out of heat and didn't come in again for six months. For-tunately for the shipper, Follansbee was a friend and boarded the dog—but of course the owner lost the use and affection of his canine buddy for half a year.

"I took one bitch to France," Follansbee said. "And she absolutely refused the male. Then, when she finally got flirtatious, she got stung by a bee. I figured that was the ball game—three thousand miles for nothing. I was ready to suggest anesthesia and subequent rape, but the dog's owner suggested a bottle of champagne instead."

As it turned out, the champagne wasn't for the dogs but for the owners, to help them though a courtship already imperiled by a bee sting. As the two men mellowed, so did the bitch, albeit in a different way, and shortly, as they say, "nature took its course."

If you're beginning to think dog breeding can drive you to drink, you're right.

We had four litters with our oldest female, Pepper, mostly to help put our son Andy through college. Then we added a fifth litter by Pepper's daughter Tess.

Pepper's first amatory outing came when she was two. Andy and I drove her to Minneapolis for her assignation with a stocky French Brit named Baron.

We were new to dog breeding and didn't have a portable kennel. The car was our PortaPet, and it began to reek like a barnyard. So did we.

Pepper was wearing black panties my wife, Marty, had designed to keep the dog from dripping all over the back seat. Females in heat do much self-maintenance, and as a result Pepper's breath would have dropped buzzards from the sky. She roamed the back seat, often plopping her paws onto my shoulder as she looked past me out the front window. She panted in my face and I tried not to run off the road and hit grazing cows.

Each time we stopped for gas, I'd strip Pepper's lacy underthings off so she could pee, hoping to God that some burly redneck wasn't at the next pump peering into our car to see what was going on. Once I forgot and paraded Pepper in her unmentionables right across the parking lot of a Quik-Stop, where a bevy of customers stood openmouthed.

It couldn't have been worse. Pepper positively flounced, as if she were proud of the damn things. I trailed at the other end of the leash, looking as comfortable as the guest of dishonor at a hanging.

The family who owned the male were strangers, and we stood awkwardly in the garage as Pepper was introduced to her Dream Lover. Baron was a stocky youngster who looked bewildered (it was his first time at dog breeding, as it was for the humans present). Pepper danced around him, tapping him with a coy paw. She was as brazen as Madonna and he was still in his Li'l Abner stage.

Females usually come into heat twice a year. The female begins dripping blood, and the period from ten to fourteen days after the dripping starts is the prime time for breeding. If all goes well she'll flip her little tail to one side and look roguishly at the male the way Mae West used to look at weight lifters. Pepper obviously was at the optimum time, for she backed up to Baron, peering over her shoulder like a long-haul trucker jockeying his rig into a narrow alley.

The theory is that the male will flex his muscles, whine sweet nothings in her ear for about two seconds, then get on with the business at paw—the quintessence of "wham, bam, thank you, ma'am!"

Baron, after looking to his human friends for guidance (and finding only embarrassed faces and averted eyes), finally let genetics rule, and shortly he and Pepper had scattered their virginity all over the garage. But passion is short-lived. Then comes the uncomfortable part.

When the male is ready to ejaculate, his penis swells within the female and traps him until the swelling ebbs enough to let him pull free. At this time both dogs want nothing more than to be separated; they are caught up in a whirlwind of second thoughts.

Baron seemed to fear the conjunction was permanent. Pepper looked at me accusingly; clearly this was my fault.

"Just hang loose," I told Baron, in a spectacularly inappropriate choice of words. "I mean, take it easy—it'll all be over soon." We stood around making small talk and tried to ignore the uncomfortable new Siamese twins.

Since then I've gotten pretty blasé about the whole thing. Pepper and Baron had three more "same time next year" encounters before we retired her from motherhood. I've also stood witness to matings by Tess, Pepper's daughter, and to the successful despoliation of several lissome lovelies by Dacques, our burly stud muffin.

Dacques's brother Chubby is a celibate who is likely to sniff a throbbing female absently, then check the food dish. He has never mated, and my wife won't let him, declaring firmly, "It'll make him *mean!*"

"No, dear," I answer. "Breeding dogs makes *me* mean."

My wife's jaundiced view of dog breeding dates from when she was forced to become a sexual facilitator for Ginger, our resident female. We wanted pups from her and Chip, my male. We knew nothing about breeding dogs.

Popular written material ignores the grimy mechanics of dog procreation. Read through the typical reportage of the romance between dog and bitch and it smacks of Romeo and Juliet, certainly not Chip and Ginger. If you're looking for gut level how-to-do-it, you're not going to find it.

So with no ready reference to hand, we headed for the vet, who rubbed his hands when he saw my old car clatter into his driveway, entertaining visions of Carribean nights. He and I have had a vacation relationship for years—he takes them and I pay for them.

"She's in heat," he announced after a series of tests worthy of the Mayo Clinic. I could have told him that: Chip, our male dog, was busy climbing the ceiling and howling like a timber wolf with his tongue caught in a food processor. For unknown reasons, Ginger failed to find this attractive and was uninterested in consummating this divine romance.

"We'll have to help her out," the vet declared, mentally adding a couple of days' beach time in St. Thomas. "Helping out" was a euphemism for assisted assault. I quickly arranged to be far out of town when the event occurred. Marty inherited the task of vet's assistant.

When I came home I was confronted by a wife and a female dog, both bristling and snarling. The mildest comment was "Never again!"

And that was from Ginger.

Dog breeding breeds rowdy stories at any gathering of bird hunters. Tell your favorite story to a group of dog owners and each eagerly will be waiting for you to finish so he can top you.

For example, three of us were grouse hunting in northeast Iowa, and we decided to reward ourselves with a good meal at the best local eatery, a dinner playhouse.

One of our two dogs was Samantha, a diminutive and saucy English setter belonging to my hunting buddy Spence Turner. Samantha was (as my young daughter once said) "having heat," but Spence and his vet conspired to defuse her through the miracle of modern chemistry.

My dog, Chip, was a lusty male Brittany, with the emphasis on "lusty." The two dogs had made the long ride north from Missouri with no apparent signs of passion and had hunted without indicating more than platonic friendship. Left alone in the parking lot of a posh dinner theater, however, they decided it was time to explore the murky depths of sexual intimacy.

"Are those *dogs* out there?" asked an incredulous waitress, pointing toward the parking lot. She was aghast, but not nearly as aghast as the procession of elegant blue-haired ladies, clad in the northeast Iowa equivalent of mink and ermine (skunk and rabbit), who, spying some peculiar activity in the graceful Mercedes in the parking lot, tottered over to see.

There is nothing so fine that a bird dog can't defile it.

BIRD DOGS are like people. They come in all shapes, sizes, and colors, with or without tails. They're intelligent, stupid, handsome, or the proverbial forty miles of bad road.

They're pointers, setters, or flushers, and they've been making up for our shortcomings—insensitive nose, limited range, and lack of endurance—for centuries. It's a bittersweet relationship, but one that endures.

Some historians trace the beginning of the human-dog relationship to about 7,000 B.C., but wing-shooting game birds didn't develop until the middle of the sixteenth century.

In 1517, Dr. Johannes Caius, of the University of Cambridge, said, "Another sort of dog there be serviceable for fowling, making no noise with foot or tongue whilst they follow the game. These attend diligently upon their masters and frame their conditions to such becks and motions and gestures as it shall please him to exhibit and make, either going forward, drawing backward, inclining the right hand or yielding to the left. In making mention of fowl, my meaning here is of partridge and quail. When he hath found the bird, he keepeth a sure and fast silence and stayeth his steps and will proceed no further and with close covered, watching eye layeth his belly to the ground and so creepeth forward like a worm."

This is an accurate if clumsy description of a bird dog in action, taking hand signals, staunch to point. But this dog's master wasn't interested in a covey flush; he didn't want to shoot flying birds. He wanted the whole covey in a net, and it was the dog's job to herd them there.

Bird netters had many tricks to keep their quarry on the ground, including flying a kite shaped like a hawk. A friend recently told me he'd heard of western hunters doing this to keep chukar partridge from flying, but admitted he'd never seen it.

Sport aside, the major reason Joe Birdhunter of 1517 didn't shoot birds on the wing was because his gun wasn't up to the job. Guns had matchlocks, and it was almost impossible to apply a sputtering match to slow-burning powder while tracking a flying bird.

So the bird hunter netted or ground-swatted his prey, sometimes slipping along beside a stalking horse—a horse or cow that wouldn't bolt when the shooter torched one off under its belly or over its back. Lacking a live stalking horse, the shooter might slink in a movable, cow-shaped blind. There was such an element of buffoonery to early bird shooting that it was a lower-class meat-gathering exercise. Not until the invention of the flintlock did "shooting flying" became an upper-class sport.

It may come as a grim shock to enthusiasts of pointers and setters, but the first bird dogs were spaniels. In 1674, Nicholas Cox wrote in *The Gentleman's Recreation* of taking partridge behind "a setting dog."

But not a setter: "You are to understand then, that a Setting Dog is a certain lusty Land Spaniel, taught by nature to hunt the Partridge . . . nay, when he is even just upon his prey, that he may even take it up in his Mouth, yet his Obedience is so framed by Art, that presently he shall either stand still, or fall down flat on his Belly, without daring either to make any Noise or Motion."

In other words, a "setting" spaniel. It probably had a long tail, because the first naturally tail-less Brittany, the only pointing spaniel, allegedly didn't exist until 1850, in the Breton town of Pontivy. Many Brits today are born tail-less, but many also are created by a vet's sharp knife.

As a Brittany owner and enthusiast these past twenty years, I've offered to make Brits out of my hunting partners' setters with my trusty Buck Stockman, but so far I have had no takers.

THERE ARE FOUR bird dog types: pointers, setters, pointing dogs, and flushing dogs. The last category includes not only flushing spaniels but also the several retrievers: Labrador, Chesapeake, golden, and a few retrieving spaniels.

Among the pointers are English, German wirehair and short-hair, and several variations. Setters include English, Irish, Llewellin, and Gordon. Pointing dogs include Brittanies, weimaraners, Drahthaars, and griffons, as well as the elegant vizsla.

All sporting dogs are a blood brew. Pointers have plenty of the hound in them, and setters and spaniels have been crossbred and re-crossbred. Regardless of breed, the dog can expose its owner to humiliation and ridicule. My favorite dog story occurred some years ago, when a Missouri forester decided to breed his female retriever to a burly male Lab owned by a fellow employee in the Department of Conservation.

The forester took the female to pick up her date in Rolla, collected the big male, and started back for his home in Steelville. The cool wind in the back of the open Conservation Department pickup kept their passion under control.

Mickey, the forester, swung onto Main Street in St. James, a small, tree-lined town about halfway home—and found himself at the end of a long parade.

It was the annual Founder's Day festivities, and the streets were jammed with people, the side streets barricaded for the parade. Ahead were convertibles with the queen and her attendants and floats featuring the latest in farm equipment. Traffic filled in behind him, and he could only press on.

Old ladies fanned themselves and thought of their lost youth. Teenagers flirted shamelessly. So did the two dogs in the back of the pickup.

The town of Steelville is still talking about the unique Conservation Department float in the Founder's Day parade.

# 6

# WORKING WITH BIRD DOGS

DOG BOOKS used to concern the fictional exploits of Lassie, Rin Tin Tin, or Albert Payson Terhune's noble collies. Now, most dog books deal with training, and there are nearly as many methods as there are books.

Hunters new to owning bird dogs fret more about dog training than about raising their kids. Maybe we all think we can raise a kid, having once been one ourselves, but raising a dog is an impenetrable mystery.

I'm still learning how to deal with dogs, and sometimes it works, sometimes it doesn't. For example, there are two ways to deal with a barking dog. One is to equip the dog with an electronic collar that gives him a shock when he barks.

My friend Spence Turner tells of an owner who tired of his dog's aimless and incessant barking and stuck a shock collar on it. He came home one day to find his dog reduced to nervous jelly while the neighbor's tiny mutt stood just outside the kennel barking—and activating the shock.

The other way is to make a dramatic statement that stays with the dog. I did this when Scout, our youngest dog, slipped into barkomania at 3 A.M. I put up with it for a few minutes, hoping he would wear down. But a dog in the grip of the barks is like someone with helpless hiccups.

I finally shouted "No!" out the open window, and that seemed to work, until I crawled back under the covers and had just gotten warm again, then the barking resumed. Scout's timing was exquisite. Each time I screamed at him he'd stop just long enough to let me get comfortable, then he'd begin again.

Finally I roared from bed, barefoot and in my shorts, and raced into the winter night to the kennel, where I proceeded to whale the hell out of the dog, who yelped a final good-bye to the moon and fled to the doghouse. The older dogs, veterans of nocturnal encounters with the God Who Lives in the House, prudently laid low.

I went back into the house dripping blood from where I'd ripped my palm taking a swipe at the dog and hitting the sharp edge of a dog feeder instead.

Dog training is not always painless.

My approach to dog training is haphazard. But my dogs are intelligent and biddable, which is half the battle. In a way they are self-training: They have the genetic tools and want to do what I want them to if they can figure out what that is.

Not all bird dogs are that way. Dogs are not people, a mistake too often made. It is wrong to think of them as "just like us," no matter how many human traits they exhibit. Of course, there is some mammalian family resemblance. Not all people are smart; not all dogs are smart. Not all people are talented; not all dogs are talented.

Stanley Coren's wonderful book *The Intelligence of Dogs* ranks seventy-nine dog breeds for intelligence. Brittanies rank nineteenth. Among the hunting breeds, Brits were beaten out by golden retrievers, fourth; Labs, seventh; springer spaniels, thirteenth; shorthairs, seventeenth; flat-coated retrievers and English cocker spaniels, tied at eighteenth. English setters tied for thirty-seventh, while the pointer came in at forty-third. This doesn't mean you don't find smart pointers or setters, but on average they don't rank among the intellectuals of dogdom. Intelligence is helpful, but there are other factors perhaps more important for bird finding. If you're in the game only to find quail, researchers show that pointers consistently have the best noses among the sporting breeds. What you give up in smarts might be counterbalanced by bird-finding ability.

NEW GUN-DOG owners sometimes wonder if they shouldn't have a professional train their dog. I tell them they can if they want, but I much prefer a dog I've trained, for better or worse, than one trained by a stranger. I'm not trying to take bread from trainers, but most trainers work with many dogs and have little patience with slow learners.

Some people simply have no empathy with dogs and probably never should own one. But if they insist on owning a dog, they are the ones who should let a trainer do the dirty work so they can hunt the dog with a minimum of fuss. They still won't enjoy the fusion of a true dog-man partnership, but at least they'll have a working tool.

My wife and I designed our house, and there are mistakes in it, but we are far happier living with our own errors than we would be living in a house designed by someone else, no matter how flawless.

I feel the same way about bird dogs. The training period is more than teacher/pupil; it is the time when the dog bonds to you and declares lifelong fealty. If a dog is trained by someone else but hunted by you, who is God to the dog? Not that a dog can't serve two masters: My son Andy and I have co-trained our dogs and are interchangeable in their eyes.

We could do far more training than we do, but we hit the essentials. We insist first on good manners. We teach "sit," "stay," and "come" early, then work on "whoa!" (the most important of field commands), "heel," and hand signals.

We insist that dogs not jump on anyone. Muddy feet are unwelcome. They all know better, but sometimes they get excited and forget and tap you with a quick paw, withdrawn so fast you can't correct them. Only the sloppy pawprint remains.

We use "okay" as a release command—the dog equivalent of the soldier's "at ease." Some use a tap on the head as a release, but suppose you have a dog on point that you can't reach—in a thicket or across a stream—and you want the dog to move and flush birds. "Okay" will work; a tap will not.

"Go on" is a frequently used command that tells dogs to quit fooling around with coyote scat or mouse runs and get to the real business at hand. Coren lists more than sixty commands that his Prince Charles spaniel recognizes.

Dogs know far more of our language than we think they do, especially if we talk to them often. They begin to associate words with situations, at least smart ones do. Every hunter knows the excitement of a dog when someone says, "Birrrrd!"

"Do you want to. . . ?" is a signal to our dogs that I'm about to ask them something pleasurable, such as ". . . find birds," or ". . . go," or something else that they don't understand, but know must be good because they've learned that "Do you want to. . . ?" is a prelude to neat stuff.

My favorite Gary Larson "Far Side" cartoon goes like this: In the first panel, headed "What the man says," a man is saying something like, "Now, Ginger, you know you shouldn't do that.

You're a bad dog, Ginger." The second panel heading is "What the dog hears," and that is "Blah, Ginger, blah blah blah blah blah blah. Blah blah, Ginger."

While I realize that it's senseless to grab a double handful of loose dog hide, haul him to eye level, and lecture him, I suspect the action more than the words has a dramatic impact on the dog's behavior. And it sure makes me feel better.

Experts say you never should lose your temper with a dog. Lots of luck. I agree that you shouldn't let every little transgression make you angry and that you should develop self-control before you ever start working with a dog. But there'll come a time when only anger will let the dog know he's broken a major commandment.

Praise is a far better incentive to good behavior than fear, but fear brings a sharp point to an important lesson.

Remember the barking puppy? There was no way I could praise him for not barking because he wasn't not barking. And the usual command "No!," which he knows as well as he knows his name, didn't work. He was caught in a night-barking frenzy and only a dramatic event would snap him out of it.

Thus entered fear—the fear that if he barked one more time or did anything other than crouch silently in the doghouse I was going to come thundering down the path to rattle his teeth again.

The fear will fade, but I hope its intimidating message will linger.

The late Richard Wolters revolutionized dog training with his book *Gun Dog* (E. P. Dutton, 1961). Wolters, a founding editor of *Sports Illustrated* magazine, devised a series of articles on the theme of "So you want to. . ." Wolters proposed one on "So you want to own a bird dog," though he never had.

He got the assignment and suddenly realized he'd better get a dog and follow through. He read all the books, thought about it, and decided convention was wrong.

"Let's set up an experiment," Wolters wrote. "Put a child in a fenced-in area when he is old enough to be weaned. Provide shelter, a bed, feed him, get a doctor when necessary, make the pen big enough so that he can run and get exercise. Then when he is seven years old turn him loose to go to school."

The fallacy that Wolters saw in conventional dog training was that trainers waited until the dog was physically mature to begin training, by which time they'd lost the vital early development stage when a dog is at its most impressionable.

I suspect the methods from any recognized dog training book will work—and there are many. Delmar Smith will tell you how to train your dog to poop on command (Bill Tarrant's *Best Way to Train Your Bird Dog*, McKay, 1984). Steve Rafe is into motivational psychology (*Birdwork*, Denlinger's, 1987). Joan Bailey teaches "conditioning," which exposes a dog to countless repetitions of what you want it to do until the lesson sinks in (*How to Help Gun Dogs Train Themselves*, Swan Valley Press, 1993). But of them all, Wolters's simple summary seems most commonsense and workable for the average dog owner.

He says, "What's required of you? Common intelligence applied every day and a will to stick to the job."

That's all dog training is. You learn to know your dog—what it will do and what it doesn't want to do, how it acts and reacts and how to deal with the problems one by one. It seems simple, but there are dog owners who are owned by their dogs. They're simply not on the same wavelength. They're indulgent or expect too much or too little; they just don't seem to understand dogs.

That figures. I don't understand simple mathematics. I would be more of a flop teaching math than I was taking it. Why shouldn't similar inadequacies plague some dog owners? Not everyone can add; neither can everyone train dogs.

I don't claim to be a great dog trainer, but I do think I understand them as much as anyone can. I have an affinity with dogs that lets me work with them effectively. I often know what my dogs are doing almost before they do it.

I live with them, and we are beyond dog and master—we are friends. We have been through Heaven and Hell together and accept and tolerate (to a point) each other's shortcomings. It's like a marriage that endures. We have a partnership, but one with recognized limitations.

The major ground rule is that the dog is subordinate. Animal rightists of course believe all creatures are equal, but animal rightists deserve to be bedded down with copperheads to see how far their egalitarianism goes.

In the man-dog equation, the dog and man share duties and pleasures, but the man gives the orders and the dog obeys them. This is a vital point to remember and insist upon throughout the life of the partnership. If you're careless with enforcing orders, you gradually build a dog that obeys some of the time, maybe most of the time, but not *all* of the time.

ANDY AND I begin training puppies on simple commands at seven weeks. By three or four months they know every obedience command I want to teach them. Once I trained a collie to "Come fore," which meant that when he was on heel and I stopped and said "Come fore!" he would circle in front and sit facing me. It was impressive, but I never could see the practical value.

A friend trained his Labrador to climb a ladder onto the roof of his house to retrieve beer cans thrown there at parties (and no, I don't know how the dog got down—I never saw the dog do it). It was a great party trick, but of limited value in a duck blind. There are far more obedience commands than there is a need to use them.

Here is what we teach our dogs, in the order we teach it:

NO: It's a sharp word that by its sound gets a puppy's attention, and if you accompany it by a scare (a tap with a newspaper, for example), any halfway intelligent puppy quickly learns what it means (even if it doesn't always obey).

SIT, STAY: These are linked commands. "Sit" is easy—just push down on the dog's hindquarters while propping up its chest with the other hand. Often a puppy can learn "sit" in fifteen minutes. "Stay" is tougher. A training table is a great help. I use an old door on sawhorses. The puppy is uneasy about being on a slick surface off the ground and looks to you for guidance. And elevating the dog is easier on the back than bending over to it. Make the puppy sit, then command "Stay!" while holding your palm upraised like a cop stopping traffic.

If the puppy breaks, put it back, command again. If it holds even for an instant, command "Come!" and praise it when it comes. Gradually increase the time the pup is on "stay" until it has the idea in mind. By the time the pup is three or four months old, you should be able to walk out of sight for several minutes before returning to release the dog.

Sometimes, just to reinforce who is boss, I'll make six Brittanies sit and stay before I open the kennel door. They're vibrating behind the open door like tuning forks. I'll even put out food to tempt them, but I insist they stay until I give them "Okay!" Then there's a Brittany explosion as colorful as a Fourth of July extravaganza. Sometimes, to make it tougher, I call them one by one.

**COME:** Two ways to do it. One is to tie a lead to the puppy's collar, wait until it's headed the opposite direction, then call "Come!" and jerk the leash (don't drag, *jerk* it) until it runs to you to escape the fright of the sudden jerk. Follow with extravagant praise. This works with aggressive puppies, but it's tough on timid ones. The longer method is to be patient and call the dog when it wants to come to you, then administer praise. Food or other incentives help attract the puppy.

Positive reinforcement works until the puppy decides there are things it would rather do than come when called. A dog that won't come is a dog out of control, and one that quickly learns it can do as it damn well pleases (and will).

I have chased down dogs that refused to come and administered whippings, then drilled them on "come" until we reestablished our relationship. Some of those sprints covered a quarter mile or more, and I've reached an age where my track days are over.

The answer in this situation is an electronic collar, which, when properly used, is the best long-range training aid ever. My buddy Spence Turner calls his shock collar Ma Bell. "You can reach out and touch someone," he says. He has rangy setters from field-trial stock, and they often are out of earshot—but not out of range of jostling electrons.

I've never been able to justify five hundred dollars for a shock collar when the roof needs work or the tax man is standing at the door. Shock collars are like not drinking. I know it's good for me, but I don't do it.

And shock collars can be devastating to a dog. Hit the button at the wrong time and you can ruin a dog or set back its development months, perhaps years. An acquaintance once electrified his dog while it was on point. The dog yawped and yowled.

"What did you do that for?" asked a fellow hunter.

"Well, he looked like he was gonna break," said the quick-trigger hunter. The dog wasn't much good after that.

WHOA!: The key field command can be taught quickly to a smart dog. As it's running toward you, leap toward it, hand upraised, palm out, shouting "Whoa!" Almost certainly the dog will stop in confusion. Continue to emphasize the "whoa" in a quieter tone, sharpening it if the dog moves. If it doesn't stop, carry it back to the "whoa" spot and firmly repeat the command, placing the dog where you want it.

It may take a while, but the dog will get the idea that "Whoa!" means stop, right now, right here. "Whoa" is appropriate for dogs that bump birds or creep on point, as well as for honoring a dog on point.

We practice in the off-season. I'll let the dogs run, then command "Whoa!," freezing everyone. We'll do it a few times, just to keep them sharp and let them know school never is completely out.

HEEL: This is a vital command. Hunters who let their dogs run free near highways are asking for tragedy. Leash the dog and command "Heel!" Jerk the leash (don't drag the dog) to get the dog in position at your left heel.

If it surges ahead, jerk the leash to stop it. If it lags, jerk to move it forward. Practice changing your direction suddenly, and stopping. If you want to impress people, train the dog to sit when you stop. You must develop a dog that will heel on command, without a leash.

KENNEL: I use "get in there," just to be contrary, but it means the same thing. Some say "Kennel up" or just "Kennel." This is an easy one to teach when you're taking the dog on a hunting trip, because the dog wants to go. It's harder to enforce when the dog is free and you want to confine it (and it knows that). You may have to enforce the command then.

HAND SIGNALS: The dog should do the grungy work of brush busting. It's not hard to teach a dog to go right or left with dramatic hand signals—in the open. It's tougher to make the dog go into nasty brush, and you'll probably have to lead the way at first.

I give a hand signal and say, "Get in there!," and if the dog doesn't move into the cover I repeat the command and get in it myself. Usually the dog follows, and I gradually withdraw from the tangle and leave the dog in it. Enthusiastic hunting dogs, once they learn that brush is where birds are, will volunteer to hunt thick cover.

DEAD BIRD: Some dogs hunt dead; some don't. I have both. I try to pair a good dead-bird hunter and retriever with one that isn't so hot. Forced training to retrieve is beyond me—I nearly ruined a dog once for *any* kind of retrieving, so I prefer to go with dogs that enjoy it.

Hunt dead or retrieve is easy training if the dog enjoys playing fetch. Throw a ball or stick, command "bring it" (my command) or "fetch," and keep it up as long as you or the dog wants to. If the dog can't find the object, encourage a hunt for it: "Look for it! Where is it?" The dog quickly gets the idea. In the field, add "Dead bird!" to the routine. After the dog has found a bird or two, it'll have the idea firmly in mind.

Those are the simple commands, all vital. If you want to fancy up your training, there are tons of others.

I haven't said anything about whistle training because I don't do it. A dog whistle around your neck is impressive to strangers and marks you as a can-do guy.

Substitute whistle commands for spoken ones. Some use several sharp whistles for "come," a couple to stop the dog so you can give a hand signal. Saves the voice, but I've just never gotten into it.

As for dog-training books, consider not just the source, but the applicability. What works for a given trainer may not suit your personality or temperament. Decide on a method and stick with it. Don't confuse the dog or yourself with a plethora of theories; stay with a simple program. Decide what you need from your dog and teach that. Pooping on command is fine if that helps you, but if it seems like a parlor trick, forget it. Both you and the dog have better things to do.

What breed of dog? Dr. Larry Myers, director of the Institute for Biological Detection Systems at Alabama's Auburn University, has done extensive testing of nasal acuity in dogs (more on this in the next chapter).

Of all the breeds Dr. Myers has tested, he rates the German wirehaired pointer tops. Also called the Drahthaar, the breed is becoming more popular all the time. (There probably are about two thousand in the United States.) It originated a century ago as a cross among the wirehaired pointing griffon, pudelpointer, stichelhaar, and German shorthair.

Wirehairs, equally at home on land and water, are one of about twenty-five "versatile" breeds, dogs that not only point birds but also will retrieve waterfowl and, by European standards, trail game and voice it, like a hound (traits which would make a pointer or setter man grind his teeth in rage). Some tend to be aggressive, and they're big enough to enforce it.

Brittanies and German shorthairs are the two most popular versatile breeds. Other breeds fairly well-established in the United States include the vizsla and weimaraner.

After hunting with Foster Sadler's sweet, versatile little Brittany, I was sold on Brits. I had three American Brittanies, and when Chip was killed by a car (bird dogs and cars are mortal enemies, and the dog always loses) I got a French Brittany puppy on the recommendation of Dave Follansbee, the first editor of *Gun Dog* magazine.

Follansbee pioneered French Brits in the United States. Of course, all Brittanies originated in France, but the earliest dogs, the American Brittanies, have become a dog as different from today's French dogs as, say, an English and a Gordon setter.

I'm not sure why, but the looks are quite different. American Brits have red noses and amber eyes; French dogs have darker noses, darker eyes. Head shape is often different as well. Black and white is a coloring forbidden by the American Brittany Club, which seems senseless chauvinism to me. Once a prospective puppy buyer said he understood that black-and-white Brittanies have better noses than orange-and-white ones. I told him coat color has no bearing on scenting acuity. I wouldn't make much of a used-car salesman either.

The American Kennel Club recognized the Brittany in 1934, the year I was born, so perhaps there is some symbolic link between me and Brits.

I've been training my own dogs for more than twenty years and have had French Brits for about fifteen. They are smart, eager, filled with Gallic *joie de vivre*, and lighten my days and my moods. Even if I didn't hunt birds they'd be a joy to have around, but the times when we prowl the birdfields together are as carefree as life gets.

Bird dogs can be a blessing or a curse, but thinking back on a quarter century of living with them, there's far more blessing than curse.

# 7

# IT'S ALL IN THE NOSE

J. L. AKE, of Maize, Kansas, uses a notepad that says "I'd rather be," at the top, and "hunting" at the bottom. In between he asks: "I was wondering if there was ever a study done on the scenting powers of upland game pointing dogs by breed. If so, which one has the best nose? Also would you address scenting conditions, temperature, etc.?"

Yes and yes.

Any creature leaves behind scent molecules as it passes, which dissipate in time. The nose of any dog can receive and process those molecules in a fashion far superior to man. "Superior" hardly begins to describe the difference between your hooter and that of a dog. A dog's scent sense is estimated to be five hundred times greater than yours, but it may be even more acute.

Reducing it strictly to quantitative differences, the human nose contains about 5 million olfactory cells, while a dog's nose has more than 200 million. (I have no idea who counted them.)

Next time your dog sneezes a spray all over your face, don't yell at him—he's just refreshing his snoot's receptors. A moist nose works better than a dry one.

Gun-dog writer Bill Tarrant told of an experiment where Stanford University researchers boiled glass ashtrays to remove all scent, buried them eight inches deep on a beach, and let two tides wash the sand. Several dogs located the buried ashtrays with 80 percent accuracy. How? Tarrant speculates that it just might be a form of extrasensory perception.

When I started asking dog experts about how dogs smell, the first answers were the predictable round of bad jokes: "Ours smells much worse when it's raining," said one. "Gee, I don't know—mine smell pretty bad sometimes," said another.

Once we got beyond that, I found there has been little research into the mysteries of dog olfaction. A German researcher, Karl Zuschneid, believes after his research on hounds that the dog's nose is far superior to a man's (which isn't exactly a revelation) and can even detect odors invisible to a gas chromatograph (which is).

"One must always take into consideration annoying and disturbing scents (human as well as domestic and wild animals). Young and minimally trained dogs are usually influenced through those annoying scents and often hindered in further tracking."

Zuschneid concludes that experienced dogs can distinguish among different scent tracks and be "scent faithful," which explains how a bird dog can trail a running pheasant through an area with many birds laying down scent tracks.

The acuity of the dog's nose also explains how it can happen on a track and follow it in the direction the animal is going rather than backtracking: The scent is ever-so-slightly stronger closer to the prey (although some experiments indicate that some dogs are confused as to direction).

Dave Duffy, a noted gun-dog writer and trainer, believes dogs learn what interests the boss rather than recognizing the scent of a new game bird through some genetic miracle. Several years back he wrote in *Gun Dog* that "hunted on a bird strange to them, many dogs will ignore the new species, categorizing it as a song bird." Bird hunter and writer Phil Bourjaily believes the same. He talks about his shorthair ignoring woodcock until it realized Bourjaily was interested in them; then he became a woodcock dog.

My experience has been the opposite. My dogs have instantly recognized such strangers as partridge, grouse, and woodcock; I feel there's a common scent to all gallinaceous birds. But my dogs also have responded to waterfowl, which certainly must have a different scent than upland birds. And they've found dead doves first time out. Is there a "dead smell" common to birds?

I've stuck quail against my nose and smelled only a faint dustiness, almost a non-odor. No one knows what that element is, except the dogs. One researcher thinks that quail scent, for example, can be broken down to its chemical components, which can be tried on dogs one by one until one or more cause a reaction, but that's an expensive and time-consuming experiment that hasn't yet been done.

The leading Doctor of Nose-ology is Dr. Larry Myers, introduced in the last chapter. Larry is a veterinarian with Auburn University, and his Biological Detection Systems group examines, among other things, examines dogs and their scenting ability.

Dr. Myers invented and markets the Smell Threshold Test Kit (SMETT), available for $14.50 postpaid in the United States from Myers. (Write to Brown-Myers, 674 Meadowbrook Drive, Auburn, AL 36830.)

Basically, the kit tests a blindfolded dog's ability to smell the test odor at various dilutions. Dr. Myers's kit not only is useful for checking Ol' Sal's nasal nimbleness before you take her to the field after birds but also is used by lawmen to check out their dope-sniffing dogs.

In the lab, the reactions of blindfolded dogs are measured by electroencephalogram. The average dog owner must read his blindfolded dog's reactions, and the dog must be quiet and calm. I've talked with a couple of dog owners who have tested their dogs, with mixed success. It works if the dog is quiet; it doesn't if the dog is frightened or uneasy.

It's enough to make a Brittany owner (me) cry, but Dr. Myers has found pointers scoring consistently high in sensitivity to odors. Not just English pointers, but the German varieties as well. He says the occasional beagle, shepherd, or Lab will ring the bell, but he also says there isn't enough raw data to make a blanket statement that one breed is consistently superior to another.

Perhaps pointers are superior in the nose because they are closer to hounds than other bird dogs. They're alleged to be descended partly from bloodhounds and have been crossed with foxhounds to improve their noses. Hounds are trailers, but a bird hunter wants a dog that wind-scents, so the ideal dog is one with the refined nose of a hound but the heads-up approach of a bird dog.

"A bird dog owner needs to watch out for the sense of smell in his dog, but that's not everything," says Dr. Myers, echoing my own feeling that the intelligent, well-trained dog with an average nose is better than a supernose with the brains of a garden slug.

Dr. Myers and his colleagues have dispelled some popular fictions about bird dogs and will work on others. "We've found that neither heartworm preventive nor heartworm treatment affects a dog's ability to smell," he says. "And that's good because we need the preventive."

Other claims are that dogs are affected adversely by auto emissions or by sleeping in cedar-shaving beds. But Dr. Myers says that "dog owners must remember that today's good dog might not be next week's good dog. Dogs are subject to a variety of diseases that affect their sense of smell. A dog might have a case of kennel cough and not even show symptoms, yet have its ability to smell affected."

Any hunter knows that temperature and humidity affect scenting ability. Other factors include how much the birds have moved, whether it's windy, perhaps even barometric pressure. There is more that isn't known about dog scenting than is.

I remember one quail season in Missouri when I thought my birds dogs had been stricken with nose paralysis. And it wasn't just my dogs. It was a rare day when hunters could claim good dog work. I watched dogs step on dead birds and fail to scent them. On the last weekend of the season, six of us with five bird dogs moved twelve coveys—and not a single covey was pointed. Either the dogs or the hunters blundered into them. We had a few scattered points, but it was far from a superior dog day. And these were experienced dogs, behind which I've hunted for several seasons.

I know these dogs were far better than they showed. What happened?

I could come up with only one possible factor: Missouri, in common with much of the country that year, was mired in drought.

I'm still not convinced dry conditions are a complete explanation. I hunted partridge in Nevada's rimrock, where it's about as dry as hunting can get, and we had good dog work. Maybe it's just that all of us hunters and all of the dogs were a year older.

Dr. Myers says no one knows if a dog's ability to smell declines with age. "It would be an expensive study because you'd have to follow dogs for years, testing and retesting," he says. "We can show that scenting ability declines with the effects of various diseases."

But nose is only part of a bird dog, and I don't think it's the most important part. The perfect dog has a superior nose, covers ground efficiently, checks back, ranges according to cover density, has bird sense, adjusts to different birds and different habitat, and probably some other things I haven't thought of.

I wish the perfect dog on everyone, but only a few hunters ever own one. The rest make the best use of the dog's tools. Which would you rather have: a dog with a superb nose that is wild and stupid, prone to bust birds, or hunt out of sight and out of control? Or a well-mannered, intelligent dog that has only an average nose?

Dr. Myers's research finds that the stone-nosed dog is fiction. "Some 85 percent of hunting dog owners have experienced what they considered to be olfactory problems with their animals at some time," he says. But he also says that true *anosmia*, the inability to smell, is very rare, and there are no recorded cases of *hyposmia*, a decreased ability to smell.

People believe nutty things about dogs, probably because there isn't enough hard research to get things straight. For example, as I've mentioned, a fellow called to inquire about some pups we had for sale. "I hear that the black-and-white Brittanies have better noses than orange-and-white ones," he said.

If I had a brain, I would have agreed and charged him an arm and a leg for a black dog, but common sense tells you that coat color has about as much to do with a dog's ability to smell as the juxtaposition of Mars and Jupiter.

Nonsense isn't limited to the uninformed. There is this chilling paragraph in *The Complete Brittany Spaniel:* "In the United States and Canada, black is a disqualifying color in Brittany Spaniels. But this offers no problem. American and Canadian dogs are totally free, hereditarily, of any gene for black. Unless someone should import a French Brittany which carries a black gene, there can never be a black Brittany in either country. As Dr. Busteed has pointed out, any Brittany in America which shows up with black is a mongrel. Should this happen, the situation should be reported to the American Kennel Club, and an investigation made so that the dog's registration papers can be destroyed."

Dr. Busteed is identified as a professor of genetics at West Texas State who bred brother to sister for fifteen generations, which tells me something right there.

Second, as the owner of several black-and-white French Brittanies (yes, someone *did* import black-gened Brits), I'd like to take the author of that scurrilous paragraph out to my kennel, where black-and-white Brits would get him down and lick him until he screamed for mercy.

All dogs are mongrels, amalgams of other breeds. A kennel owner should breed for traits that are desirable for the dog's given mission, not because of fashion or fad. He should breed for intelligence and nose, not coat color. When bird-dog owners start worrying more about how pretty their dog is instead of how well it performs in the field, the world's game birds can start to rest easy. One more predator will have been neutralized.

COMPUTER OWNERS with access to the Internet and the World Wide Web don't lack for information on dogs, just the time to absorb it.

The World Wide Web has several dog home pages. Check these out: http//:tamvm1.tamu.edu/~GUNDOG-L/. This is a huge list of discussions about gun dogs. A general page with dog info is http://www.zmall.com/pet_talk/dog-faqs/lists/www-list.html. Field trialers can roost at http://dog.isdn.net/field.htm. Setter owners (English, Irish, Gordon) can make contact through email: hkruse@mail.eworld.com.

Here are three breed addresses: vizsla at listserv@power mac.inacom.com; German shorthair, http://www.whc.net/gsp; and weimaraner, http://www.eskimo.com/~chipper/weim.html. A good link for hunters in general is http://www.wolfe.nct/~hunter/, which has links to other hunting pages.

This is just a surface scratching. You'll find much more if you want to spend your hours at a computer rather than in the field. There is software to generate dog pedigrees, vet schedules, and a host of other dog-related paperwork (costs about $120).

Speaking of vet schedules, all hunting dogs need certain shots. Some hunters cheat on this, and they suffer (for example, taking a chance on heartworms or Lyme disease). It costs to keep a dog, but the emotional cost of losing one to a disease that could have been prevented is (or should be) far worse.

An indispensable part of keeping your dog healthy is to keep its vaccinations up-to-date. Below is a table that shows all the major vaccinations (at minimum) that a dog in the U.S. should have. Conditions in your area may necessitate additional shots; ask your vet about them as they may not always be routinely included in normal shot programs. DHLPP is a combination shot: Distemper, (canine) Hepatitis, Leptospirosis, (canine) Parainfluenza, (canine) Parvovirus.

| AGE | VACCINE RECOMMENDED |
| --- | --- |
| 5–8 weeks | DHLPP |
| 9 weeks | DHLPP plus Corona Virus |
| 12 weeks | DHLPP (2nd shot), 1st lyme |
| 4 months | Rabies, Parvovirus, 2nd lyme |
| Annually | Boosters on above diseases |

Other vaccines and preventives include heartworm pills, beginning about at five months (or earlier in warmer climates). We use the once-a-month pill. There is also a chewable daily tablet. A friend treats his dogs with carefully measured ivermectin, but I'm afraid I'll make a mistake, so I pay more and get a laboratory-measured dose.

Lyme disease shots are an annual affair and highly recommended if you live or hunt in states where deer ticks are common and Lyme disease is present. My home, Missouri, isn't much of a threat, but on my last grouse hunt in Minnesota I picked numerous deer ticks off the dogs (all of which had been vaccinated).

Lyme disease is a threat to both dog and man, one of several tick-borne diseases that we once didn't know about and now do. Lyme disease has become the nonfatal disease of the decade, replacing herpes. It's a toss-up as to which disease is more fun in the acquisition—hunting and Lyme disease or whatevering and herpes.

Besides Lyme, ticks carry babesiosis, Colorado tick fever, ehrlichiosis, relapsing fever, and two unsettlingly common and nasty diseases, tularemia and Rocky Mountain spotted fever.

Dogs can contract Lyme or babesiosis, ehrlichiosis, Rocky Mountain fever, and a disease whose name alone is enough to make a dog vomit: haemobartonellosis.

Rocky Mountain fever is most common between mid-April and mid-September—when hunters aren't afield. It's a dangerous disease, and the symptoms (as is true with all the tick-borne diseases) mimic many common ailments (fever, chills, headache, and abdominal pain, plus a possible later rash).

Lyme disease often creates a "bull's-eye" rash at the bite site. Symptoms are typically flu-like. Preventive shots have been available for dogs for several years, and if you're going to be hunting in tick country, check with your doctor—a human shot was nearly perfected at this writing.

I've known a couple of people who've had tularemia and am convinced I don't want it. It hangs on and can have long-lasting, debilitating effects. Tularemia has typical flu-like symptoms, and you can get it not only from ticks but also from the classic carrier, rabbits, usually by cleaning one that's diseased. But I also know a fellow who contracted tularemia when he stuck his hand with a broken leg bone from an infected pheasant.

Ehrlichiosis is a disease of my home country, the Ozark Plateau. It dates only to the late 1980s as a recognized boogeyman.

I know hunters in both Missouri and Arkansas who claim to have gotten Lyme disease, but I suspect they actually had ehrlichiosis. One symptom, in addition to the usual chills, fever, and headache, is weight loss, so I guess fat people *could* run naked through tick country, but I wouldn't recommend it.

How do you know if your dog is tick-sick? Clinical signs are similar to those for humans, except the dog can't tell you it has a headache. Watch for arthritic behavior with Lyme disease, hemorrhaging of mucus membranes in Rocky Mountain fever.

The other diseases have minor deviations in symptoms, but the bottom line is that if your dog acts sick, it is, and should be taken to a vet as soon as possible. Tell the vet that you've been in tick country.

Better, get a Lyme shot and spray the dog (and yourself) with a good tick repellent. (Check with your vet to get a good one that won't wash off easily, since dogs are forever getting wet in the field.)

And don't let fear keep you out of the field. There are dangers from ticks, snakes, lightning, and windstorms, not to mention hypothermia, sprained joints, broken bones, and a host of other potential evils. So what. Your house may unaccountably collapse on you while you're watching *Wheel of Fortune*.

As my gardening sweatshirt says, "Compost Happens."

THERE ARE OTHER vaccines and preventives, but there's no point in medicating the dog if there's no problem.

Find a vet with a hunting background, or at least one who knows hunting dogs. Some vets are large-animal specialists or lap-dog doctors. Better to have one who owns a Lab or shorthair and sometimes shoots at flying creatures.

Checking periodically for worms is vital. Most vets make it part of an exam when you have the dog in for shots. Puppies should be wormed at two to three weeks and again at four to six weeks.

Some heartworm preventives also knock out other worms. Again, check with your vet for recommendations. Routine worming, done by some dog owners, is a shotgun approach to a problem. Why worm if it isn't necessary? Here's a table that can help you decide.

| WORM | SYMPTOMS |
| --- | --- |
| Roundworms | Pot belly, dull coat, vomiting, diarrhea, loss of weight |
| Hookworms | Anemia, diarrhea, bloody stools (especially puppies) |

| | |
|---|---|
| Tapeworms | "Rice" on anal area or in stools, possible diarrhea or vomiting |
| Whipworms | Loss of weight, some diarrhea; difficult to detect |
| Threadworms | Profuse watery diarrhea, lung infection symptoms (especially puppies) |

---

YOU'LL HAVE far less trouble with worms if your dogs are on concrete runs. Even then, frequent and thorough cleaning of the runs is vital. Besides, it's disgusting to let your dogs tromp around in their own waste.

Fleas and ticks are common. Sprays and dips work for a while, but my dogs spend much of the summer swimming in the lake, and it's tough to keep a spray on them.

We haven't had a flea problem for several years, since the dogs are isolated from flea-carrying fellow dogs (except when we go hunting; then I keep my fingers crossed that my fellow hunters have their dogs flea-proofed).

Dog ticks are the Missouri state insect, so we have to deal with hundreds of them every spring and summer. I spray during the worst times, handpick them the rest of the time. Bluegills love ticks.

SNOOPY NOTWITHSTANDING, the ideal doghouse doesn't need color television and a fully equalized stereo system. It does need to provide the dog with protection and a modicum of comfort. One fellow I know, who cherishes his dogs, still provides them no bedding. The dogs sleep on bare boards. The floor, however, is double-insulated against Minnesota winters, and the house is built inside a garage, with access to runs on the outside.

Anywhere the winters are fairly cold, which is most of the country, a doghouse should be insulated and have a wind baffle, a short inner wall that creates a corridor or vestibule, behind which is a sleeping chamber protected from wind coming in the door.

Metal spring-loaded doors that snap shut after the dog enters are available, but the dog has to be trained (or train himself) to open the thing with his paw. Some people get away with a piece of carpet or canvas or other material tacked to the top of the door, through which the dogs can push in or out, but this is neither particularly airtight nor very durable.

With the possible exception of chain mail, I can't think of a material strong enough to resist the carbide-tipped teeth of a Brittany with nothing else to do all day but reduce his accommodations to shreds. One set of young dogs, eight months old at the time, chewed the inner walls out of their doghouses because they found the foam insulation inside wonderful fun to shred. I had to rebuild two houses, gnawed as if by a colony of beavers. Bird dogs and teenagers are the only two species known to destroy their own nests.

My dogs now have cedar log houses. I cut five- to six-inch eastern red cedar logs and chinked them with insulation sealed with mortar, then inserted three-quarter-inch plywood walls inside. They may chew their houses, but it'll take a while to destroy them.

My favorite bedding is cedar shavings because it makes the dog smell wonderful and, it is alleged, the essence of cedar also discourages fleas. Some maintain that the pungent cedar aroma garms up the delicate machinery of a bird dog's nose; others say possum muffins. I don't know and the dogs aren't talkin'.

A compromise is to use the shavings through the nonhunting part of the year, perfuming the dog when he's at his most gamey, and switch to native grass hay during bird season. Native grass is far superior to straw: It doesn't shred to dust and sharp particles that can lodge in a dog's eye.

I have a little mini-prairie of switchgrass, big bluestem, and Indian grass that I scythe each winter to provide bedding for the dogs. Veterinarian Tom Holcomb, who writes a good column for *Gun Dog*, favors prairie hay over cedar shavings, too. But if you leave hay in the house too long, the dogs crush it to dust, just the same as straw.

The answer, of course, is to change the bedding periodically. You don't sleep on the same sheets year-round, do you?

You do? Remind me to hunt upwind.

# 8

# THE BEST QUAIL GUN?

BY COMPARISON, religion and politics are noncontroversial. Every hunter has a set-in-concrete idea of the perfect quail gun. And all are right, of course. A good quail gun is one with which you consistently hit quail, one you like and feel comfortable with, whether it's an antique Sears autoloader or a Purdey.

For the record, I believe in side-by doubles, but that's purely because of their aesthetics, not because they're any "better" than pumps, automatics, or even over-unders.

Some hunters prefer a side-by's broad sighting plane; others are distracted by it. Bob Brister, a competition shooter, gun instructor, and longtime gun editor of *Field & Stream,* says, "I'm accustomed to the single sighting plane of an over-under or gas-operated gun and seem to hit better with 'em. So, I suspect, do most Americans."

Charley Waterman, the dean of upland bird writers, says, "Like other bum shots, I have tried to find a gun I could hit quail with, using several over-unders and one English side-by-side." He's settled on a quail gun that isn't even a quail gun: a Browning Model 425 Sporting Clays, in 20 gauge with a 28-inch barrel. "I guess it's a Citori by breeding. The 425 is ported and I had a Kick-Eez recoil pad put on it because the pad has a rounded top that doesn't catch in my dog-whistle string, suspenders, or shirt collar. This gun has screw-in chokes; skeet and modified are my pick for bobwhites."

Another friend, Jim Dean, the longtime editor of *North Carolina Wildlife* and a lifetime quail hunter, likes an old 12-gauge Fox A-grade double that belonged to his father. "Dad let me play around with some truly nice Parkers, Lefevers, and Foxes with the idea that I could pick one," Dean says. "I initially settled on a 20-gauge A-grade Fox with 26-inch barrels because it was light, handsome, somewhat rare, and its original straight stock seemed to fit me."

Most upscale hunters would have slobbered over this little fairy wand, which had everything going for it, including the weight of history.

"Alas," Dean says with Shakespearean regret. "I couldn't hit squat with it."

His 12-gauge Fox has been refinished and the barrels may have been shortened, so to a collector it's basically worthless. To a quail hunter, however, it's priceless. "I can actually hit quail with it, and I've gotten so cocky shooting clay birds that I challenge my son Scott to set the trap at odd angles while I walk ahead with the gun slung over the elbow—which is the way I encounter most bobwhites anyway, since our dogs have always enjoyed a good joke."

Like a growing number of hunters, Dean appreciates the history of gear as well as its efficiency. "When I'm wearing a vest and pants that are nearly fifty years old (they were my grandfather's) and carrying a shotgun that was manufactured before I was born, I can almost fool myself some days into thinking that nothing has changed."

The outdoor writer Charley Dickey, who has hunted quail since God's Own Dog (the French Brittany) was a Spanish spaniel, is the ultimate pragmatic hunter. "I've never been a shotgun queer," he says. "I thought the Model 21 should have been used on carriers to catapult aircraft. I've never slept with a Purdey nor made love to a Churchill. I think a shotgun should hold three shells, else how can you dream of shooting a triple?

"You don't want a shotgun that weighs seven pounds in the morning but ten pounds at dusk. I own one quail shotgun, a Remington Model 1100 semiautomatic—20-gauge, improved cylinder, 26-inch barrel, with a ventilated rib. The 1100 catches lint and dust beetles and is inclined to jam two or three times a season. When it does, I talk my buddy into cleaning it in the field. If it happens to go all season without jamming, I clean it in March."

In my youth, the old quail hunters of Chariton County often put down three birds from a covey. Most used autoloaders but some had pump guns, and it took a fast hand to shuck three shells before a covey got out of range. I do well to get one and fire at a second bird within range with my double.

My friend Dave Mackey has tripled with his autoloader, but as he ages he doesn't do it as often. He's the only one among my regular hunting pards who uses a three-shooter. My late best friend Foster Sadler grew up hunting quail with a 20-gauge Winchester Model 12 pump, choked full—a waterfowl gun. The Model 12 is a wonderful gun, strong as a tank (and in 12 gauge about as heavy).

Foster was among the best quail shots of my hunting circle, but his Model 12 full-choke would be neither the choice of many hunters nor the recommendation of any expert. Still, it was what Foster could hit quail with, and it was a sad day when a house fire destroyed that gun.

Like most hunters, I have strong preferences. I'm mostly Methodist, mostly Democrat, and all double. Which makes me a target for half the population at least. Feel free to disagree, but here's what I like in guns, loads, and accessories.

## A SIDE-BY DOUBLE

It looks nice, it's traditional, and it provides a wider sight plane on which to rest the bird, which gives me a feeling of confidence. Its two shots are plenty for me; a third shot is wasted for all but the fastest and best quail shots.

My ideal quail gun is a 20-gauge, with barrels 26 or 28 inches long, whichever feels better. A longer barrel tends to be heavier in front and will swing a bit more smoothly. That's one reason waterfowl hunters and trap shooters prefer barrel-heavy guns. A short, light-barreled gun with its mass toward the rear is quick and responsive but jittery to aim—better suited for point-and-shoot hunting like grouse or woodcock.

The stock should fit, and if possible a gunsmith should make the measurements. I like a splinter fore-end rather than a beaver-tail, though my current shooter has a thick beavertail and I'm used to it.

## CHOKES BORED IMPROVED CYLINDER AND MODIFIED

Some opt for skeet-skeet, which translates to no choke at all. That's fine if all your shots are ten to fifteen yards and if you hunt only quail with that gun. Most hunters have a limited gun cabinet and can't afford a specialized gun for each species. The solution is either interchangeable choke tubes or a compromise boring. Improved cylinder and modified is the most widely endorsed upland compromise.

On his doubles, Bob Brister normally chokes his barrels improved cylinder and modified but sometimes opts for improved modified for the second barrel, "so I can take my time and nail the second bird on out there a piece if necessary. Old as I'm getting, it sometimes takes a while to locate flying objects."

## NO. 7 1/2 WINCHESTER HUNTER LOADS

I shoot these for almost everything—a fine all-around upland load. If you consistently shoot behind birds, try No. 6 steel shot; it's faster than lead and may compensate for your sluggish follow. But remember that most quail shots require no lead (that's "leed," not "led") at all. You'll shoot under quail more often than you'll shoot behind them.

My hunting buddy Spence Turner sometimes gets in slumps and resorts to No. 9 shot, on the theory that the more pellets you put in the air the more chance of hitting something. Sometimes it seems to work. If you're in pheasant country, No. 7 1/2 will kill any close-in rooster, but try a first barrel of No. 7 1/2 Hunter and a follow-up of No. 6 high-base.

Charley Waterman's load of choice is 7/8 to one ounce of No. 8 shot for bobwhite and Mearns' quail. The larger quail call for one ounce to 1 1/8 ounces of No. 7 1/2 shot. Waterman loads his own.

Charles Dickey mostly shoots low-brass No. 8 shotshells. "If some nines are left over from dove season, I use them for quail. Sometimes late in the season I may use No. 7 1/2 high brass."

Bob Brister prefers pigeon load No. 8s with 1 1/4 ounces of shot if he's after meat, but prefers light loads: "One-ounce 12-gauge loads such as the 'handicap'-type American traploads in 8s or 7 1/2 s or the faster International-style 24-gram (7/8 ounce) or 28-gram (1 ounce) loads. Probably that's because I'm used to quick loads at sporting clays, but the added velocity seems to shock quail better. Even with the 28-gauge I'd much rather have a little 3/4-ounce load cracking out at nearly 1,300 fps than the one-ounce 'overload' that gets only about 1,100 fps."

Brister sometimes shoots skeet 9s in close cover, but prefers 7 1/2s overall "because they just seem to get fewer cripples."

## A GOOD HARD CASE

This protects the gun on trips, but it's bulky. A proper case must lock, and if you're shipping it by air, tape the end locks with duct or strapping tape. I've never lost a gun permanently with the airlines, but I wouldn't ship a gun that couldn't be replaced (like my L. C. Smith). For day trips, a well-padded soft case is fine. I know a hunter who keeps a nice 20-gauge Browning Sportster uncased behind the seat of his pickup and it looks like it fell off a garbage truck. "What's a nice gun like you doing in a place like this?" I murmured when I saw it.

"What'd you say?" he asked.

"Nothing," I replied.

THE CHOICE OF GUN depends on what you expect to get out of a quail hunt. Brister says, "Heaven forbid I'm ever caught with only one quail gun to blame, even on a desert island. But the decision would come down to whether I really needed a sack full of quail or simply wanted to enjoy the pleasure of a light-carrying, sweet-handling little gun."

His choice for the latter would be a Beretta Model 687EELL 28 gauge with 26-inch barrels and Briley choke tubes. "This is a little wand of a gun weighing less than six pounds, but is really not as difficult to control as it sounds."

But Bob says if he were out to load the game bag (and the daily limit in Texas, where he lives, is fifteen), he'd go with a light-weight 12-gauge gas-operated autoloader—a Browning Gold or Beretta 303.

"If the terrain required a bit more speed of handling (or a whole lot of gun carrying between coveys) I'd probably shoot my Browning Gold Hunter with 26-inch barrel. I also have a Beretta 303 20 gauge with 26-inch barrel that just seems to hit for everybody. I take it as a backup gun for guests who get discombooberated by our quick south Texas quail."

Brister thinks the trend is definitely toward single-sight–plane guns. "In years past I shot mostly doubles at close-cover woodcock and quail, but having shot competitive sporting clays so much in recent years (and seen even the English switch to over-unders and even autoloaders for that difficult test of all-around shotgunning), I suspect there ultimately will be less snobbery involving even the lowly gas guns. Also, the carbon burners don't kick nearly as much, and I don't need any more retina detachments."

THE THEORY AND application of choke has confused bird hunters for years. Most know what choke is and roughly what it does, but beyond that, choke is a mystery.

Fred Kimble, an Illinois market hunter, supposedly invented the idea of squeezing the muzzle of a shotgun to constrict the shot string about 1870, but there were choked shotguns long before Kimble.

The English gunmaker W. R. Pape patented a system of choke boring in 1866; however, according to W. W. Greener, whose book *The Gun* dates to 1881, choke-boring existed in the 1700s. Some credit Jeremiah Smith, an 1820s-era gunsmith from Rhode Island, with the introduction of choke. Whatever the origins, choke has been around longer than any living shotgunner.

Choke constricts the shot charge, thus giving a denser pattern at a longer range than would a more open choke or no choke at all. Too many gunners think of choke as a way to extend the killing range of a gun. Except when attempted by the rare expert, long-range shooting is an invitation to cripple. A tighter choke should be insurance that you kill a bird at normal range, rather than crippling it.

Upland hunters almost always overestimate the range at which they shoot, while waterfowl hunters underestimate their range. Since almost all upland shots are in the range of fifteen to twenty-five yards, upland hunters should use chokes that give a wide but still effective pattern at these close-in ranges.

Here's where the double-barreled gun has an obvious advantage: The first shot can be with an open choke and the second with a tighter choke. Single-barreled shooters limited to a single choke can compensate somewhat by loading the magazine with a light load of small shot, perhaps No. 8 or 9, for the first shot on grouse, woodcock, and quail, followed by a high-brass load of No. 7 1/2 or No. 6 shot for the second shot.

There are different types of built-in chokes: English, American, swaged, recess (or jugged), and bell (or reverse). English and American chokes are the only ones commonly encountered. Unless you shoot expensive English doubles, you'll encounter only American choking.

PATTERNING A shotgun is something everyone needs to do and intends to do, but somehow never does. It's a classic case of traveling down the well-known road to Hell—the one paved with good intentions.

A quick way to check the choke of your barrel(s) is to shoot off a rest at a center mark in a thirty-inch circle at forty yards. Full choke will put 70 percent of the shot in the circle, modified 60 percent, improved cylinder 45 percent. Improved-modified should shoot 65 percent. Cylinder, or no choke at all, should shoot from 25 to 35 percent. Skeet 1 is roughly equivalent to cylinder boring, while Skeet 2 is slightly more open than improved cylinder. The differences are slight.

Of course you need to know the number of pellets in the shot charge to figure percentages. That varies with load and gauge, but any gun shop will have a chart showing the various combinations.

Another way to check the effectiveness of your gun on your chosen game bird(s) is to draw a life-size picture of the bird (anatomical accuracy doesn't count) and shoot it at your usual range. Would the pattern actually kill the bird? Are there holes in the pattern? Will different loads and chokes give a better pattern?

Although one pellet in a vital area will kill a game bird, it usually takes several, depending on the size of the bird. The more centered the shot pattern, the more chance there is to lodge those lethal pellets. If you're shooting birds with the edge of the pattern, you're asking for cripples or misses.

To add a little confusion to the mix, remember that the pattern you see on a pattern board is not the pattern a flying bird encounters. That bird is moving, and the shot load is not at the same point in space at the same time but strung out. Relatively few of the shot intersect the bird; the rest pass in front, behind, below, or above. Only a stationary bird, like a turkey, is equivalent to a pattern-board target.

Aside from not knowing the characteristics of their shot patterns, many hunters don't know if they're aiming where the gun actually shoots. They assume the shot charge is going where their eye tells it to, but if the barrel is bent, it may not be. It doesn't take much to throw the pattern off. Then the answer is to use Kentucky windage, have a gunsmith straighten it, or get a new barrel. But you need to pattern the gun to find out.

To check point-of-aim and impact, divide the pattern sheet in quadrants and center the shotgun bead on the target, just as you would a rifle. Shoot from a firm rest. Now count the pellets in each quadrant. They should be roughly equal. If one quadrant is heavily weighted, you're shooting off in that direction. If most of the pellets shoot high or low, you have a problem that way.

EVER SINCE the first choked barrels, hunters have been faced with the problem of adapting their existing chokes to different game birds. You can own a closetful of guns with differently choked barrels, you can buy a slew of barrels for a single gun, or you can opt for a mechanical method of changing chokes on one barrel.

S. H. Roper actually patented a screw-in choke in 1866, but it took many decades for the idea to catch on. Among the first was the Cutts Compensator, an external set of chokes that screws onto a barrel. The Poly-Choke works much like the nozzle on a water hose, screwing down to tighten the choke, loosening to open it.

Both the Cutts and Polychoke were cumbersome external appendages as ugly as a knee-length cast on Miss America. Today's screw-in choke systems, from manufacturers such as Hastings, Winchoke, Remchoke, Briley, and Tru-Choke, are virtually invisible and fit factory-threaded guns or guns that have been retrofitted. No one should thread a valuable old double, but most modern guns can be retrofitted for choke tubes. This opens up the possibility of more than a dozen chokes, far more than any hunter ever will need. Finding the right several is the key, which is complicated because different guns pattern differently, even with the same load and choke. Further, steel shot patterns differently than does lead. You should shoot a more open choke with steel than you would with lead to get a similar pattern density at a given range. Even among lead loads there is variation—copper-plated versus straight lead, for example.

It's not as frustrating as it may seem. For one thing, ammo is much cheaper than barrels or even choke tubes. Find the choke tubes appropriate for the type of shooting you do and pattern them with your favorite load. If it isn't satisfactory, try a couple of different loads—maybe up or down a shot size or a slightly hotter powder charge (or one less powerful). If that still doesn't give a good, consistent pattern, spend another twenty dollars for a choke tube either one size tighter or one looser, then pattern again. Sooner or later you'll hit the ideal combination for your gun.

You may spend a hundred dollars before you're satisfied, but that's cheaper than a new barrel and you'll have a gun that delivers a killing pattern. Any misses are your fault. Of course this kills the familiar excuse for missing: blaming the gun.

Most upland hunters with single barrels choose either modified or improved cylinder, though some opt for Skeet 2, which is slightly more open than improved cylinder. Waterfowl hunters traditionally go with a full choke and turkey hunters choose extra full, or they get into the esoteric world of choke tubes that squeeze a shot charge even more.

Shotguns begin to get load-sensitive at modified choke and get more so as the choke tightens. "Load-sensitive" means that a given load (shot size and shell length) may not pattern well with a tight-choked gun, but a shot size larger or smaller might do just fine.

A hunter who uses the same gun for upland and waterfowl might be satisfied with an open choke tube for upland and a tighter one for waterfowl. But there are different types of waterfowl and upland hunting. If the shots are long, the choke needs to be tighter, and you might find a hunter using the same tube for long-range pheasants or prairie grouse as he does for duck hunting over open water. If the duck hunting is close-in over decoys, the hunter might use the same tube for both teal and quail.

Most choke tubes should only be hand-tightened and can be removed without a wrench, but Remington choke tubes can back out with heavy loads and need to be tightened an extra tug. No choke tube should be overtightened; there's the danger it could cut right through the barrel. And don't lubricate the threads of a choke tube; oil can jam the threads. If you're uncomfortable with bare metal, use a dry lubricant.

TO SOME EXTENT, good shooters are born, not made: They have the hand-eye coordination and other physical attributes that make some people basketball stars and others spectators. But practice improves any shooter, regardless of native ability. And practice, coupled with good shooting habits (gun mount, concentration, follow-through, and so on), improves a shooter even more. Add to this a gun that fits the shooter and a choke-load combination right for that gun and you have an optimum situation.

Until, of course, a bird flushes in an unexpected direction, dips or flares as you shoot, or the sun gets in your eyes. Considering the variables, it's a wonder we ever hit anything.

Shooting is an art, and I'm no artist. Never have been, never will be. My shooting faults began early and dug deep. If I shot often during the off-season I'd get better, but I'll never be a good quail shot. That's an unpleasant truth, like facing the fact that you're not really good-looking or don't understand automobile mechanisms.

My goal is to shoot one hundred quail in a season, not to satisfy a bloodlust but because it would indicate two things: There are plenty of quail, and I've magically become a better shot than I've ever been. My best in the years since I've been keeping records was slightly over fifty birds. Last season it was forty-seven. With three weeks to go in the season as I write this, I've shot fourteen birds.

This year's low kill has less to do with poor shooting than with a lack of targets. My shooting has been pretty good; my bird finding terrible.

Quail populations come and go, but my shooting has a depressing consistency—much like my golf game before I found I could throw the club farther than I could hit the ball and gave it up. One day I'd fungo vicious slices, the next day wicked hooks that looked like a Nolan Ryan curve ball.

Once I hit a ball into the middle of a highway; fortunately there was no traffic, because I heard a joke about a guy who hit a ball through the windshield of an oncoming car, triggering a twenty-car pileup. "Do you realize what you've caused?" thundered an irate policeman at the golfer. "Massive damage, blocked traffic, people hurt all over the place. What are you going to do about it?"

And the golfer replied, "Well, I thought I'd move my right hand a little farther over on the club."

The moral is, you can't correct faults that won't hold still. After more than forty seasons, I've worked myself out of the beginner's tendency to flock-shoot. I pick a bird, concentrate on it, bring the gun up smoothly, swing through—and miss. Then I'm so flustered at seeing a dead bird still flying that I miss a hastily jerked second shot.

It's not as if one hundred birds is a Himalayan goal for a serious bird hunter. Missouri's current season runs seventy-six days— November 1 to January 15, with a daily limit of eight. A hunter out every day and killing a limit could bag 608 quail. No one does, as far as I know. But say you hunt three days a week in a ten-week season. That's thirty hunts. If you only get half a limit each time, that's 120 birds.

I *do* hunt three days a week and sometimes I do kill half a limit. But more often it's one or two birds, and the season total is considerably less than one hundred. In 1990 I killed fifty wild birds in eighteen hunts and probably another twenty-five to thirty pen-raised birds on hunts in North Carolina and Georgia. I had one hunt with a limit of wild birds, another where I killed six.

In 1991 I hunted more but killed fewer—forty-four quail in thirty-one hunts. I had one limit hunt but quite a few where either I didn't move a bird or I missed the ones I did move. My average season runs to slightly more than forty quail. But one year I killed only fourteen quail—1984, the year of the dreadful winter.

Snow fell in mid-December 1983 and stayed on the ground for nearly two months. Temperatures plunged, and the combination of inaccessible food and bitter temperatures decimated Missouri's quail. It took about four years for the birds to recover. No wonder my 1984 season was poor.

Serious quail hunters will laugh at my statistics, and I certainly don't point to them with pride—or with any accuracy, either.

The average shooter takes 3.1 shots per bird, according to one study. But I know many shooters who are nonplussed if they miss *any* good shots on quail. Remember Nash Buckingham's Art of Restraint.

Good quail shooters don't take doubtful shots, and they make the rest. Given that, creating that 3-to-1 ratio takes quite a few sub-par shots. It's a rotten job, but someone has to do it.

I remember one hunt when I bettered the ratio, but that's sort of like a basketball player who hasn't hit a three-pointer all day throwing one in from midcourt to win the game. I killed three birds in seven shots, but I had a double on my last two shots. I was one for five going into the last covey flush. I'd missed two pointed birds that flew straight away in the open, two shots each. Then a covey got itself caught in the open, feeding in milo stubble. I walked between the crouching birds and their escape route, a ditch. They panicked and flushed right in front of me, and I dropped two just as neatly as Mr. Buck ever did. My two astonished Brittanies, who had plunged past the covey downwind, whirled and came back; each fielded a dead bird en route and brought them to me, wondering who the hell fired those shots.

They knew it couldn't be me.

THE JOY OF HUNTING lies in the process itself, not just in getting a limit. But the occasional limit is an undeniably keen pleasure.

In my ideal quail hunt, birds move often enough to support an adrenaline high, keeping me from feeling the leaden fatigue of a birdless trudge; there's good dog work, and a few good shots are mixed in with the ones I expect to miss. I'm happy with three or four birds. They entitle me to membership in the club. No birds leaves you a frustrated bystander with no money at the craps table.

Given my acknowledged mediocre shooting, who am I to advise on either shooting or shotguns? Well, Miller Huggins was about as big as Babe Ruth's bat, and he told the slugger how to hit. Same here.

I know what needs to be done; I just can't do it with any consistency.

Shooting to a point is a matter of habit. To shoot well, you must practice pointing the gun until the mount and track are automatic—developing muscle memory, it's called. By constant practice, a right-handed basketball player can learn to go left. But doing anything with the off-hand is tough—whether it's eating or shooting layups. And side dominance isn't limited just to hands.

DO YOU KNOW which is your dominant eye? Or even that there is such a thing?

You could be handicapping yourself in the field if you're try-ing to shoot with a nondominant eye. My son Andy is a right-hander with a dominant left eye. He copes somehow and shoots better than I do, but he would have been better off starting to shoot left-handed.

*The Orvis Wing-Shooting Handbook* (Nick Lyons Books, 1985) is the only instruction manual I've found that covers in any detail what author Bruce Bowlen calls cross-dominance. Bowlen prefers that students learn to shoot from the dominant-eye side. In other words, a right-handed shooter with a left-dominant eye should learn to shoot from the port side. This is the preferred solu-tion of every shooting expert I know.

In most people, the dominant eye corresponds to the domi-nant hand; in other words, a right-handed person will be right-eye dominant and a lefty left-eye dominant. But those who are cross-wired have a problem. If you shoot right-handed and have a dominant left eye, for example, your left eye will point the gun several inches off-target—far enough to almost ensure a miss. Shooting with a built-in error is no way to consistent success.

It's simple to find your dominant eye. Just point at any object with your dominant hand and both eyes open. Assuming you're right-handed, shut your left eye. Your finger should still be on tar-get if your right eye is dominant. Now shut your right eye. Your finger will be pointing to the right of the target if you're right-eye dominant.

Another method is to cut a small circle in a sheet of paper and, with both eyes open, line it up on an object some feet away, using the hole like the peep sight on a gun. Assuming you're right handed, shut your left eye. The object should remain centered if you are right-eye dominant.

Try it a half dozen or more times. You should get the same result each time. A few people don't have a consistently domi-nant eye. Eileen Clarke, a Montana outdoor writer, is one. "I checked it some years back, and every time my right eye was dom-inant," she says. "But a couple of years ago, I started missing birds.

I checked again and every other time I tested, my dominant eye was different—one time the right eye, the next time the left eye."

Eileen got help from Bill Dowtin, a Flagstaff, Arizona, gunsmith. Dowtin has worked with many "cross-dominant" shooters and believes there are only two viable solutions: You can switch shoulders and shoot from the dominant side, or you can close the dominant eye before the shot. In Clarke's case, he used a third solution: obscuring the vision in the dominant eye enough to force dominance to the other eye.

You can learn to shoot from the off-side. Tom Gresham, a gun writer and shooter, is cross-dominant. He recommends keeping an unloaded shotgun at hand and practicing in every spare moment for as long as it takes. "People can change their shooting side even as adults," Gresham says. "Easiest way is to shoulder the gun on the 'correct' side every few minutes. Do this every day for a couple of months and it starts to feel natural."

Tom's father, the gun writer Grits Gresham, noticed Tom's cross-dominance when Tom was young. "He quickly switched me to shooting left-handed," Gresham says. "The thing to watch for is a shooter leaning his head over the stock to use the 'wrong' eye for sighting."

Gresham estimates that about 10 to 12 percent of the population is left-handed but somewhere around 20 percent is left-eye dominant, which means quite a few people have a cross-dominance problem. He thinks left-handers with right-eye dominance are few—but I've talked to some, so the problem exists on both sides.

New shooters shouldn't have much problem adjusting, but old dogs probably will have trouble learning to shoot from the offside. Dennis Carpenter, an archery coach from Washington State, says, "I've worked with eye patches with some success, but if shooters are serious about improving beyond average, I always recommend switching hands to match the dominant eye."

Orvis's Bowlen also suggests as a solution shutting the dominant eye at the moment of shooting. "The shooter can use both eyes until the last instant," he says. "Only after the decision to shoot has been made and the gun starts toward the shoulder is the eye closed."

But Bob Brister thinks that with some shooters the sight picture is so fixed that they'll continue to point the gun where their dominant eye told them to even with that eye closed. "You should shut your eye before you ever see the target," he says.

And some people simply can't close one eye. They either have both eyes open or both shut. So the closed-eye solution won't work for them.

It goes against good gunnery to shut one eye while shotgun shooting. Keeping both eyes open and concentrating on the bird is the nub of successful shotgunning—but that's only when the eye and hand work together.

Dowtin's solution for Eileen Clarke—obscuring part of the dominant eye or blurring its vision enough to force the other eye to become dominant—doesn't work with everyone, but most shooters respond. A bit of transparent tape on the dominant-eye lens of their shooting glasses blurs vision and causes the dominant eye to stumble and hand the baton to the other eye.

Brister once ran into a cross-dominant shooter at a meeting and improvised a solution by spitting on the fellow's lens, then sprinkling dirt on the slobber. Crude but effective.

His method is to mount the gun on the shoulder of a buddy or over a tree limb so you don't have to use the leading hand. Close the cross-dominant eye and get a proper sight picture with the eye you want to become dominant. Then shut that eye without moving the gun.

Grease the forefinger of your free hand with something—Vaseline, hair grease, whatever. Move your finger in front of the lens until it obscures the gun barrel and dab the grease on that spot of the lens. You later can apply Scotch tape or a shooter's aid called Magic Dot to the inside of the lens so it won't come loose.

Now you have a permanent fog that should force your dominant eye into submission. It's an aggravation—any eyeglass wearer knows how irritating a blur on the lens is—but it may solve the problem.

Eyes change as we age. Bob Brister says, "Of all the problems I see among shooters who are reasonably competent, eye changes are the most common. A shooter who was strongly right-eye dominant when he was younger starts to get some eye changes, and the eye that doesn't have all that gun mass in front of it wants to take over and start running the show." Brister has had a couple of cataract operations and finds that when his eyes get tired, dominance will switch to the off-eye.

The most expensive solution to the problem of cross-dominance is what's known as a crossover stock, a specially made stock that bends (casts) enough to point the gun properly even though the cross-dominant eye is trying to force it off target.

Theoretically it should work. But Bill Dowtin doesn't think so. "I've made stocks for twenty years," he says. "And I've seen no evidence that a bent stock will correct the problem. Your dominant eye will pull those barrels off the target. I don't know how much is conscious and how much subconscious, but the dominant eye will take over and ruin the shot."

Only very good gun makers have the skill to build a successful crossover stock, and it will cost far more than buying enough ammunition to learn how to shoot from the other shoulder.

While starting all over goes against the grain of every shotgun shooter, it's better than muddling through life shooting several inches off-target every time.

RECENTLY, I SHOT a round of sporting clays, with predictably poor results. There were plenty of challenging and interesting shots— I shot down on crossing birds from the edge of a ditch and fired at settling birds over water and took birds launched from behind as they crossed over my head—but almost none duplicated the typical quail shot.

Crazy quail, if it still exists, apparently was much fun (I never shot it). A rotating launcher in a pit threw birds in different directions depending on where in the cycle the bird launched. You could get one going away or coming straight at you, you were never sure where—just like real quail shooting.

Sporting clays is the golf of shooting, a walkabout setup on a manicured path to different stations that utilize terrain and try to duplicate hunting shots. The station names are descriptive: Springing Teal, Bounding Bunny, and so on. It isn't upland hunting, of course, nor can it be, not without the partnership between hunter and dog. You don't bust brush and brave briars to get from the Darting Dove to the Settling Woodcock.

Some sporting clays setups duplicate quail shooting fairly well. One dandy is a launch of about five targets with one "poison" bird of a different color. The idea is to shoot a double without breaking the poison bird.

Trap and skeet shooters lock into a rhythm and pattern because they know every bird will be exactly like the last bird thrown from that trap at that station, discounting wind or light conditions. Not so in sporting clays, where the speed and size of the birds can vary and where the traps can be moved to give great variety to the shots. In this way it's a little more like hunting.

Why shoot clays? For the fun? Obviously. For the competition? Probably. We are a competitive nation, and competition lurks behind every activity that starts out as fun. To sharpen off-season shooting skills? Certainly. A round or two of clays is far better than skeet or trap just before the hunting seasons open, but you can do the same thing cheaper with a hand trap or a portable trap and a buddy to throw birds.

In England, sporting clays is considered the fastest growing participant sport, which it probably is here, too (since hunting, fishing, and golf have pretty well reached their saturation levels). "Sporting clays attracts many people who don't hunt or want to shoot live animals, but who enjoy shooting," said my late friend Arthur Shepherd, who was an English sporting clays instructor. "You'll see entire families, including Grandma."

A round of sporting clays is expensive in this country. Most courses charge at least twenty-five dollars and often more. Sometimes the charge is by the hour rather than by the round. A fast shooter could fire a hundred times in an hour. Brian Bilinski, credited with building the first United States clays course in Houston, says he once crammed as many shots into an hour as he could and fired 125 times, but what fun is there in racing the clock?

For that matter, what fun is there—at least for typical upland game hunters—in the competition that has come to dominate the sport? What began as an off-season exercise to keep shooting eyes sharp now suffers from the same problem that afflicts every recreational pastime ever created by Americans. We can't seem to enjoy an activity without forming a league and offering trophies.

Because a clays course tries to be all things to all hunters, it has stations that call for tight-choked guns and stations that demand open chokes. Clays enthusiasts say that your hunting gun should be able to break every target on a typical course, and that's true—but specialized guns or choking arrangements do it better, and today's competitors increasingly go to these technological solutions.

The moment you begin gunsmithing on the course, you've gone beyond simulating a day in the brush and gotten into the gadgetry associated with competitive shooting.

IN 1973, The Orvis Company set up a shooting school and sent several instructors to England to learn how it's done there. They came back with layouts for shooting courses that included a duck tower, wobble traps, and movable traps.

A decade later, Brian Bilinski, the manager of Orvis's Houston store, was in England and shot on a course set in a natural environment. He'd been told to begin a shooting school in Houston, but he decided to expand the idea. His would be a course with stations, open to the public (as opposed to the shooting school, which was open only to students), and it was profit motivated. "The reason for the whole thing was to generate traffic back to the store," he says.

Bilinski combined what he'd learned in England with his college training in setting up fitness trails to come up with a walking clays course. "The fitness trails use bark mulch pathways through the woods and have stations where joggers can stop and do different exercises," Bilinski says. "I did all the design and layout on a ten-acre piece of ground on a leased ranch.

"The fields were not that technically difficult. What made them different was that there were trees around. That was the most eye-opening part. When the shooters came off the course, they were smiling from eye to eye," Bilinski says. Sporting clays had its first foothold in the United States. It has since come of age, with courses at most gun clubs and magazines devoted exclusively to the sport.

Still, as much fun as sporting clays is, I'd rather hunt real birds with dogs. Like field trials, clays is an artificial substitute for the real thing.

I have no problem with those who enjoy field trial or shooting clays. As long as it's fun, it *is* fun. But when it becomes competition, to my mind it subverts the intent of the exercise.

# 9

## THE WELL-EQUIPPED BIRD HUNTER

I AM A CONNOISSEUR of brush, having submitted to its caresses for fifty years. I know the stuff that hurts you the most and am wise to Nature's most obnoxious tricks. I just can't seem to do anything about it. As I type this my wrist is dark with dried blood, the legacy of the afternoon hunt.

But we found two coveys, the dogs and I, and we killed three quail. So what if it took a couple of rips from wild rose and a stab on the pate from a honey locust? What's a little blood among mortal enemies?

Among the woodland perils, the forked stick is the most diabolic. You trudge through the brush, bone tired and looking forward to a hot bath and bed, when it catches your foot in its crotch, the long end digs into the ground and begins to pivot, and momentum carries you forward with your foot trapped somewhere behind you, waving frantically on that devilish pivot point.

You are going ass over teakettle, no doubt about it.

And then there's the lubricated rock, perfectly round, slick as a greased ball bearing, deposited here by a glacier several million years ago for just this moment. As you fling your $2,500 shotgun in a wild attempt to keep your balance, one of two things happens: Either your gun lands on the rock, causing $2,375 worth of damage, or your knee does, creating a limp that will plague you for months and send your orthopedist on an extended Caribbean vacation.

Brush is where game lives. Thick brush is where much game lives. Theoretically, the dog does most of the brush busting, but inevitably you must follow Buster into the thicket. He'll be on point in the rough or he'll roust birds that fly there.

Everything in Missouri wears spurs—catbriar, wild rose, blackberry, locust, sensitive briar, and some stuff no one has named because they can't get close enough to it. Forging into a Missouri quail thicket is like swan diving into rolls of barbed wire.

There are three tools that ameliorate the savage caress of brush: 1. clothing, 2. shooting glasses, 3. locator collars. The first two are for you, the third for both you and the dog.

## CLOTHING

Two items are necessary for protection: boots and britches. A good pair of boots is vital for several reasons: first, to keep your feet dry, and second, to protect them from sprains and strains.

Actually, there's a third reason. The proper sole protects you from a disastrous slip. I once threw a shotgun halfway across a gully when my feet went out from under me on dry leaves. A different sole would have given me more traction. My hunting pard Spence Turner once spent three days of a four-day, thousand-dollar bird-hunting trip to Oregon laid up with a sprained ankle.

Choice of boots is as variable and individual as is choice of gun. I prefer leather boots, but I find the combination of Gore-Tex uppers and leather bottoms wears better and provides superior ankle support. I prefer lug soles for traction, but they are heavy and gum up in muddy conditions.

I suspect there are several "perfect" boot styles, depending on what you do. (You'll need two pairs, in part to adapt to different conditions but more important so you'll always have a dry pair.) You can get by with a comfortable featherweight leather boot if you're in easy terrain. But if you hunt brush and briars, you need something tougher. One hunter told me that he wore out a Cordura-faced boot in one day in brush. Leather is much tougher for bottoms, but Cordura is fine for uppers. Likewise, lug soles are great for rocky hunting, not so necessary in snow or mud. And if you're blocking on a pheasant drive, insulated boots feel great, but they'll be hot if you're walking.

John DePalma, who worked for Irish Setter boots, says, "The number-one ruiner of boots is our own sweat. The temperature inside the average boot is 120 degrees. We sweat a cup of water into our boots in a day's hunt. It has to go somewhere. Pull out the foot bed (the insert in the boot). To dry boots, lay them on their side—air gets in better. If you can, lay them on a rafter, better yet because hot air rises. *Don't* use hair dryers. They're too hot. For foot comfort during the day, carry a couple extra pairs of socks and change during breaks in the field. Buy boots with top-grain leather. Split-grain is not as good. Thinsulate uppers breath moisture out. If it's 30 degrees or higher you probably don't need insulated boots. Be sure you know whether the boot calls for silicone or other boot dressing. To silicone, put the boot upside down on your hand. You want the silicone to flow up the boot, not down."

Unless you're that rarest of quail hunters, the nude predator, above your boots will be a pair of pants. Hunting pants are usually made of nylon in a variety of weights, depending on what you need. Open-country hunters need only lightweight nylon-faced brush pants, while those in thorny brush need something tougher.

You can get bib overalls in a heavy cotton duck fabric or denim (Carhartt makes the best) and have the legs faced with nylon, which provides water resistance as well as wearability.

The advantage of bibs is that you're not constricted by a belt around the waist; they also retain upper-body heat where you need it most—your torso. I like the feel of bib overalls; I think that bibs, faced with briar-resistant fabric, are perhaps the best choice of all.

Aside from nylon, you can face pants with duck (a tough cotton fabric) or Cordura, a Du Pont fiber that is extremely rugged but heavy.

Browning and others make "waxed" cotton poplin clothing (waxing is a waterproofing treatment). I don't like the feel of waxed material, and you have to rewax it periodically.

Avoid insulated clothing. Quail hunters generate plenty of British thermal units, and I've never hunted in such cold weather that I needed insulation. If you must warm your legs, wear modern thermal underwear that will wick moisture away from your skin and keep you dry but warm.

The alternative to bibs or pants is chaps. Compare perhaps twenty dollars for chaps to three or four times that for the other choices. Further, chaps are extremely portable. Stick them in your shell vest and put them on as needed.

More and more I find myself wearing chaps over a pair of blue jeans as opposed to the several pairs of brush pants I own. Chaps, like pants, come in different weights for different conditions. Some are lined with Gore-Tex or water-repellent nylon to keep them waterproof.

There also are snake-proof chaps for the faint of heart, made by Thomaston Mills (brand name Rattlers). Wick's carries them (see below). They're about twice the cost of regular chaps, and most snake strikes will be turned by a boot anyway (besides which you're probably more in danger of lightning strike than snakebite).

Hunting shirts are a matter of choice. I like cotton chamois cloth shirts but have worn wool. Woolrich makes good shirts of both materials. Other material choices include soft canvas (good-looking and long-wearing) and denim (makes you look like the Marlboro Man). Other hunters prefer a tee shirt topped with a hooded sweat shirt (this is good in cold, windy weather—the hood should be ample enough to cover your hunting cap).

Most of the season in most of quail range will be sufficiently clement so that a shirt and perhaps a sweatshirt is enough, but in really cold weather, a lighweight windbreaker is ideal. I can't recall ever, in any state, needing a true, lined hunting jacket. Always a windbreaker with underclothing, all topped with a shell vest, has been plenty warm.

My windbreaker is a rain jacket compact enough to fit in my shell vest, always available if it rains or becomes cold and windy.

I don't like gloves because they interfere with the feel of the safety and trigger, but if it's cold, you need hand protection. I often compromise by wearing a warm glove on my left hand, a lighter one on my shooting hand. Lightweight deerskin or suede gloves provide protection from abrasions and briar rips but not much warmth.

Ski gloves are designed to give warmth to a hand gripping a ski pole (or a gun), but they are fairly bulky. The tighter the fit, the better you can feel your gun, but the more your blood vessels are constricted and the colder your hands get.

Gloves with Thinsulate lining are lightweight, not terribly bulky, and a good possibility—try them on for fit and feel.

Cabela's (800-237-4444) offers a forty-dollar "shooting glove" of Cordura shell, Thinsulate, and Gore-Tex insides, with a streamlined index finger that is supposed to slip easily into a trigger guard.

Gloves are a compromise. The best glove combination I ever had was army issue, an inner liner glove of wool topped by a shell glove of leather. Together they were warm, and it only took an instant to slip off the outer glove on my trigger-finger hand and stuff it into my vest. Of course, that presupposes a nice point rather than a wild flush. Sometimes that even happened.

All my hunting clothing comes from Wick's Outdoor Works (806 S. Sturgeon, Montgomery City, MO 63361, 800-325-2112). John Wick is a coonhunter who tired of wearing out clothing on his midnight rambles and decided to design his own. His clothing proved so popular with bird hunters that he added hunter-orange shell vests and other accessories. His chaps are the best on the market. He also carries Carhartt clothing, which is just as tough.

Clothing from Wick and Carhartt is blue-collar. It is not stylish and doesn't have that sleek gloss of upscale outdoor clothing lines. But it wears, and that should be the criterion by which hunting clothing is measured, not how good you look in it.

## SHOOTING GLASSES

Shooting glasses are expensive (perhaps $150 for a good pair), but what is your eye worth? Shooters are particularly prone to eye damage. Even dust from a clay bird can blow back into a shooter's eye.

Brush always goes for the eyes, and I was stung several times before I wised up and began wearing safety glasses.

Shooting-glass lenses are made of three materials. In order of desirability they are polycarbonate, CR 39 resin, and crown glass. The first two are less than half the weight of glass. Polycarbonate and resin scratch easily, and when you're looking at the world through $150 glasses, rose colored or not, you don't want to do it through a disconcerting scratch.

Polycarbonate and CR 39 can be coated to make them more scratch resistant. If you're wealthy, this is the way to go. CR 39 is more common among hunters because of the combination of cost and effectiveness.

Your shooting glasses should provide UV radiation protection. Ultraviolet radiation is a cause of corneal inflammation and can lead to cataracts. It can also cause eyelid tumors and basal-cell cancer. No one is immune to UV radiation, and blond, blue-eyed people are the most susceptible. Exposure is additive—it builds up like a bank account, only not as benignly.

What about lens color? For most situations, clear lenses are fine. Some hunters (myself included) opt for a yellow lens, but any tint will decrease the amount of light entering the eye and theoretically inhibit vision. None "gathers" light (which some shooters believe). There is a cost.

Yellow filters out some gray tones and make a dark object somewhat darker. A quail stands out against its background better with a yellow lens than it would with none or a clear lens.

An orange tint (called "target orange") probably will help clay-bird shooters because it makes the bird stand out. The most popular hue is Light Medium Target Orange, or LMTO. A new hue for target shooters is light purple, which makes clay birds stand out against dark backgrounds.

So-called blue-blocking lenses are supposed to enhance your low-light vision, but eye experts feel a clear lens with ultraviolet protection does a better job. Blue blockers affect color perception and also depth perception—neither problem welcome to an upland hunter.

Polychromatic lenses, the ones that darken or lighten according to light conditions, are a mixed bag. They never completely lighten, so they may be a problem in very low light conditions.

There are several frame styles for shooters that keep the glasses high on the nose and out of the way of a gunstock. Randolph and Decot are two manufacturers, Lehman another. Some frames allow lens change (Lehman offers a quick-change design).

Other shooting-glass options include antireflective coating (increases the amount of light reaching the eye to 99 percent in a clear lens), antiscratch coating, ultraviolet protection, tinting, polarizing, polychromatic ability, different frame and lens materials, and prescription lenses.

Shooting glasses, like any competitive equipment item, are confusing and even contradictory. Find a pair that does what you want and offers UV protection, and add any other options you think are necessary. Take good care of them with a hard case, and if you're lucky you won't close the car door on them as I did with an eighty-dollar pair.

Human vision is almost a subjective thing. Some shooters either see better or think they do with certain hued glasses, and whether it's actual or psychological, those shooters should go with those tints.

## LOCATOR COLLARS

The locator collar, commonly called a beeper, is an electronic unit about the size of a roll of silver dollars that mounts on a collar and emits an intermittent signal when the dog is moving but a steady one when the dog goes on point.

The obvious advantage of a beeper over the old traditional bell is that a bell doesn't make any sound when the dog points. There are two other possible advantages: I think the beeper makes the dog steadier, because it learns you will come when the steady signal starts. And there may be a confusing effect on game birds that freezes them in place.

I can't prove either theory, but observation and gut feeling tell me they are true.

Most locator collars are beepers, after the sound they make. But one sounds like an English police car and another a hawk scream (theoretically to keep pointed birds on the ground through fear of the raptor).

There are several brands on the market, ranging from a low-end price of about $50 up to about $150. All use 9-volt batteries; some are economical with juice, others eat batteries like I eat popcorn.

The original Tracker Collar, invented by Dave Lunn, an intense Minnesota grouse and woodcock hunter, still is durable and cheap, but there are improved designs and models. Lunn has become increasingly indignant as others have poached on his design, but he also has steadfastly refused to alter the original, which has several problems: The battery wires are fragile, the battery is difficult to remove, and the top of the battery is exposed to corrosion and rust.

Still, Lunn deserves much credit for inventing a tool that I wouldn't be without. I've had one Tracker for more than ten years, and it's still working (though Lunn figures four to five years is a good lifespan).

The original and some imitators have the sounding unit slung under the dog's jaw. While I've never seen any evidence that the sound bothers dogs, it makes sense to have the piercing signal away from the dog's ears, not directly beneath them. Newer designs have the sounder mounted on top of the collar and the battery unit underneath. Other advantages of this design are that snow seldom clogs the sounder and the sound isn't muffled by the dog's body.

My current favorite is the Lovett, which slings the battery case beneath the dog's throat and the sounding unit atop the collar. Lovett offers a conventional beeper or a hawk call in varying signal configurations.

## THE BIRD HUNTER'S VEHICLE

I've been bird hunting for more than forty years and have driven to and from hunts in everything from a Model A to a Mercedes. It seems that each new hunter I meet, from the partridge chasers of Nevada to the bobwhite devotees of the Midwest, has settled on the same vehicle as the ultimate Bird Car.

I speak of the Chevrolet Suburban, and I mention it by name rather than by type, because there has been only one like it for several decades; (although Ford is introducing a competitive model).

At present I have a small Nissan pickup; it's okay, but it's not a Suburban. I traded our Burb after 190,000 miles, not because it was mechanically worn out but because it was rusting, and I couldn't believe it would last forever. A friend had a Burb with 250,000 miles on it and sold it to an acquaintance who, as far as I know, is still driving it. The only reason I didn't get another one is that I couldn't afford it.

I don't know if the Burb is overpriced or not (a new one's well over $30,000). The last suitable hunting car before the Burb was a 1967 Ford Fairlane station wagon that cost $2,800 new and got twenty miles per gallon until the day it died. It had a big engine, plenty of room, and, in its declining years, a decrepitude that made it suitable only for a scruffy bird hunter. My Burb struggled to get thirteen miles per gallon, and if I ran the air conditioner that dropped to about ten. Oil magnates worldwide broke into smiles whenever I picked up my keys.

I bought the Burb used with 70,000 miles—more than I wanted, but it was the only one I could find. Used Burbs are scarce because people tend to hang on to them (one friend has two—a new one and one with 250,000 miles). If you shop around, you should be able to pick up one less than five years old with 50,000 miles or less for about $12,000 to $15,000.

Get tinted glass—it's easy on the eyes and makes it tougher for thieves to see what you have inside. And by all means get dual air conditioners, which are more efficient than a single conditioner (but run them as little as possible: they wreck your gas mileage).

Burbs offer three back-door possibilities. Ignore two: the power-window tailgate and the hand-cranked tailgate. Suburban tailgates weigh enough to give Arnold Schwarzenegger a hernia. Get double doors.

When you find your Burb, take care of it. Be sure to lubricate the constant-velocity joint when you grease the Burb, and periodically repack the hubs and take care of the front differential. Use 30-weight oil in the summer, multigrade in winter. Change the transmission fluid every 25,000 miles.

I seldom use four-wheel drive, although I did learn to appreciate it on a cold day in Nevada, when we were about fifty miles from the nearest help and the road thawed, leaving a greasy film as slick as deer guts on a doorknob.

The Burb is strictly my choice for the proper bird hunter's vehicle. Make your own decision. The sport-utility market is glutted with boxy little four-wheel-drive vehicles, and many are used by bird hunters, but none (in my opinion) has the versatility of the Burb. The family car certainly won't cut it. Muddy, slobbering dogs and Mother's church dress don't mix. (Just ask Mother.)

The other choice in a birdmobile is a pickup with a camper top, which is what I now have. It's acceptable, but inconvenient compared to the Burb, where everything is in the same compartment. My camper top has side windows that raise, a nice feature that makes it easy to get at the truck bed's contents. If you're limited to rear access, anything toward the cab end of the truck bed is difficult to reach.

Either a Burb or a pickup will hold two of the largest dog crates side by side at the back end and a third in the middle if necessary. That's enough to hold six dogs, and any bird hunter involved with more than six dogs doesn't need a vehicle; he needs an exorcism.

## DOG FOOD

They say those little balls of fried cornmeal got named hush puppies because they were tossed to the ol' hounds to quiet them.

Typical. If it's table scraps, Bowser will love it. Maybe so, but he probably won't thrive on it. A couple of my dogs are whacko for cabbage, but I wouldn't recommend raising a puppy on cole slaw.

Neither would the Purina Pet Care Center, the research facility of one of the nation's largest dog-food manufacturers. I took a tour of the place some time back.

There are a thousand dogs in residence, a constantly rotating camp for dogs sprawling across 330 acres near Eureka, a small town outside St. Louis in the Ozark foothills. There's a long waiting list for Purina bird dogs because, even if they couldn't point a quail on a pool table, you know they've been well cared for.

The dogs test both Purina foods and those of their competitors and, when they've demonstrated whatever the testers want demonstrated, the dogs go home with a new owner—maybe a hunter or a just a pet lover.

The Purina facility opened in 1926 and has worked with twenty-eight breeds over the past sixty or so years. Many are hunting dogs—pointing dogs and retrievers—but others are pets such as schnauzers or working dogs like huskies.

Susan Butcher, a four-time winner of the Iditarod, the 1,150-mile dogsled race from Anchorage to Nome, is a Purina consultant and feeds her winning team on rations jointly devised by her and Purina's team of nutritionists—a marketing coup on par with a sneaker company nailing Michael Jordan to sell gym shoes. "What you feed during the race isn't that important," says Dave Bibiak, the center's nutritionist. "It's what you feed the rest of the year."

Incidentally, for dog owners who despair of their pup ever realizing its heritage, Butcher's famed lead dog, Granite, was one she wanted to give away and couldn't because no one wanted him. The dog blossomed at three years old and now is a legend.

I'm always leery about mentioning products or companies, because for every good company there are several other good companies—and good public relations doesn't necessarily a good company make.

But the basic information put together by Purina and its competitor, Alpo, is invaluable to a hunting-dog owner. Publications by both companies are exceptionally helpful and largely without commercial interruption; they offer good information without an objectionable sales pitch. You can build a good doghouse or a kennel run with their plans, and the house won't even have their name on it.

And you can learn plenty about dog nutrition. Experienced nutritionists at both Purina and Alpo not only test their own company's food but also keep an eye on the competition's food. It's like Ford and Chevrolet. If one gets something better than the other, you can bet the other will have it pretty quickly.

And that's a good thing. Dog owners benefit from the competition, and from the major companies' major expenditures on development and quality control.

I'm not saying the Big Two make better dog food than anyone else, but I'll guarantee it's as good as you can get short of some incredibly expensive vet's diet, usually reserved for dogs in special circumstances, not for hunting dogs.

Cutting costs by feeding something mixed at the local feed store may help your wallet, but you won't be doing your dogs a favor. We watch our own diets; we owe it to our dogs to watch theirs, too.

It's easy to measure the nutritive efficiency of a dog food— if you can stand the test. Feed the dog a measured amount with a known nutrient content (i.e., protein, fat, and so on) and collect, dry, and measure the same elements in the waste matter. "It gets pretty rank around here when we're baking dog waste," says Mary Fuller, associate nutrition manager at the Purina center.

Nutritive efficiency is only one factor in the usefulness of a dog food, though. It helps if the dog likes the stuff. Dogs respond to taste, aroma, and the physical characteristics of food, just as we do. A dog likes something wonderfully chewy because he's a meat-eating predator by heritage.

Another factor to consider in dog feeding is the amount the animal eats. "The greatest single nutritional disorder is obesity," says Bibiak. "You can almost literally feed a dog to death—kidney failure is the most common cause of death in older dogs and obesity is a contributing factor."

So not only do you need a dog food that tastes good, smells good, and feels good to the dog and that meets its nutritional needs, but you also need one that isn't too high-powered for the dog's metabolism.

Dogs in condition actually eat less than those lounging around the kennel, getting soft (and fat). Purina has proved that by working dogs on a treadmill, day after day, for weeks (the dogs enjoy it, incidentally) until they're in peak shape. Once there, they eat less than they do when they're getting into shape. And they use the food more efficiently, as measured by fecal analysis.

Here are a few simple facts on dogs and feeding that I picked up at Purina:

1. Adding warm water to almost any dry dog food just about triples its palatability. (I use a self-feeder, which eliminates the possibility of adding water.)

2. Meat is no good as a source of calcium and has few vitamins. Calcium as an additive, however, is not helpful and may block absorption of trace elements into the dog's system.

3. Some hunters believe in giving a dog electrolyte-replacing fluids, such as Gatorade, but they are useless for a dog because dogs don't sweat and so don't lose electrolytes. Excess electrolytes actually can depress a dog's performance. Cool water is best to cool the dog. Use a bicyclist's squirt bottle for quick shots of water.

4. Panting is a dog's most efficient cooling device, and it's less effective on a humid day because there is less evaporation.

5. Dogs in condition have a lower body temperature. The higher the body temperature, the quicker the dog becomes exhausted.

6. The most stressful time of a dog's life is during reproduction.

7. Beware of labels that stress Total Digestible Nutrients (TDN). Most are overstated.

8. Moist dog foods (including canned) are eagerly eaten by dogs—but you're paying for the water content; not only is canned dog food high in cost but also it's nearly 80 percent water, compared to about 12 percent for dry dog food.

9. Puppy chow is specifically designed to give a grow-ing dog what it needs *while it's growing*. A puppy can have serious diet problems if it's fed on regular dog food. Fat puppies, like fat kids, aren't desirable.

10. Bargain dog foods usually aren't: The ingredients may not be the best and the quality control may be inef-ficient. You might get excellent food from a small or low-cost manufacturer—but your chances are best with a manufacturer of known reputation.

THE PURINA PET Care Center has a series of excellent leaflets, free for the asking, from Pet Care Center, Checkerboard Square, St. Louis, MO 63164. Subjects include: Story of Purina Nutrition Research, Comparing Pet Foods, Supplementations May Be Haz-ardous to Your Pet's Health, The Importance of Palatability and Digestibility, Meat and Bone Meal, Obesity, Protein, Tips to Help Prevent Insects in Grain-Based Foods, What Pet Food Labels Tell You, Caring for the Aging Pet, Kennel Construction and Man-agement, How to Select a Puppy, Housebreaking Puppies, A Good Start for Your Puppy, Dog Feeding: Puppies, Dog Feed-ing: Reproduction, Feeding the Adult Dog, Feeding the Hard-working Dog, Grooming Your Dog, Traveling with Your Dog, Kennel Plans, Dog Breeding.

There also is a series of Kennel Tips on controlling internal parasites, kennel drainage, kennel sanitation and rodent control, building a whelping box, tattooing, cold-weather care, feeding and watering equipment, warm-weather care of dogs, controlling external parasites, and building a dog house.

Alpo also has a pet center and brochures of interest to dog own-ers, including: The Dog, Stress and Your Dog, Small Animal Geri-atrics, Canine Nutrition and Feeding Management, Perspectives on Canine Obesity (hear that, Pepper?), Diarrhea in the Dog (yes, you, Chubby), Feeding and Training Dogs for Hard Work, Pets on the Go, Feeding for Breeding, Puppies, Parents and Kids, and If

Rover Could Read (facts on dog food and dog-food labels). The address is Alpo Petfoods, Box 2187, Allentown, PA 18001.

We tend to mistrust big companies, figuring, rightly, that they are mostly interested in selling us their product. But both Purina and Alpo's informational bulletins give good value and avoid the hard sell.

On the other hand, you could flip Fido another hush puppy and hope for the best.


## HEALTH

Quail hunting is hard work. My hunting pard Spence Turner has more tape on him at day's start than an NFL interior lineman. And at day's end, he hurts about as badly. Spence's morning taping ritual usually begins before daylight so he can be mobile when the rest of us groan out of bed.

Aches, sprains, bruises, strains, and abrasions are the constant companion of the hard hunter. Once I fell over a fence and rammed my elbow into a tree. The arm hurt for a while, then began to get better—until I woke in the middle of the night with the entire arm throbbing, swollen, and red. I usually avoid doctors like rattlesnakes, but it was apparent this had gone beyond home health care.

"My God!" my doctor said. "You have blood poisoning." He gave me a massive shot of antibiotics and a tetanus shot and told me with ghoulish relish of his two previous patients with blood poisoning: "One died and the other was crippled for life."

Very encouraging. Fortunately, I recovered, but it scared the hell out of me. "Carry a tube of Neosporin with you," the doctor said. "Any cut or abrasion, use it."

And I do.

I probably have more medical equipment for the dogs than for myself, but it doesn't hurt to have a small first-aid kit, especially if you're away from home. While doctors advise against using antibiotics except for prescribed ailments, I used leftover pills once after Dacques, in a fight with another dog, mistook my hand for his opponent's throat. It hurt like hell, but I immediately cleaned the wounds, dosed them with peroxide, and popped antibiotics for a couple of days—watching anxiously for red streaks.

I got better.

Once I intercepted a ricochet pellet with my thumb knuckle. It didn't break the skin, but my thumb hurt for months. Another time the hunter next to me was hit in the cheek by a stray pellet from an out-of-sight hunter. Another hunter I know took pellets from a fellow who couldn't see him.

No one I hunt with is likely to shoot me at close range, but the stray pellet is always possible. Accidents happen. You can fall through ice or into a deep ditch. You can get ripped by a barbed-wire fence. The potential for disaster is almost limitless.

So carry first-aid gear for yourself. And the dogs.

I've never been bitten by a venomous snake, nor have any of my dogs (one apparently *was* bitten by a nonvenomous snake he ran across), but I know people who have, and I have been along when dogs encountered rattlesnakes.

My dog Chubby once killed a northern water snake when he accidentally stepped on it while investigating what the other dogs were barking at. He leaped straight up when he felt the snake move, grabbed and shook it in a blur of motion, and threw it into our lake. The snake, its back broken, sank. No harm to Chubby, but what if it had been a rattler?

You can snakeproof your dog by using a defanged rattler and a shock collar—aversion therapy—but that's beyond the capabilities of most hunters. Most of us take our chances.

It's usually cold enough when I'm quail hunting that snakes are dormant, but southern hunters are often afield at the same time as snakes. Of them all, the copperhead is the most prevalent and least venomous.

Porcupines and quail seldom if ever coexist, but I suppose there are a few places where the two cross-habitate. Either a dog will attack a porky or it won't. Mine have pointed them a couple of times but haven't yet challenged them to a fencing duel.

Skunks are not exactly a health hazard (unless someone threatens to beat you bloody for bringing a stinking dog home), but they are common. Some of the commercial de-skunkers work pretty well, so I'm told. I've had only one dog-skunk encounter, and I dunked and shampooed the dog until it was tolerable, then kenneled it outside until the aroma wore off. A vet or vet supply house would have de-scenters and directions on use.

## DEAR DIARY

I've kept a hunter's diary, log, journal, whatever you want to call it, since 1984, and I curse myself for not having started one when I began hunting.

Chronicling the day's events has become an after-hunt ritual. After the dogs are fed and tended, my gun is clean, and so am I, I'll have something to eat, a shot of something close by, and my boots off; then to the journal, followed by a few pages of a good book and a solid eight hours' sleep.

There isn't much of moment in most entries, but I try to capture more than the hits and misses. How was the weather? What did we see other than game birds?

My first entry, November 1, 1984, was opening day of that season. It's a dull bit of writing, about as noteworthy as a shopping list. My son Andy and I found two coveys and I killed one bird.

But it's memorable to me because two of the three dogs on that hunt are dead, including Ginger, who pointed the bird I shot. Guff, my dearest friend for a dozen years, retrieved it and later pointed a woodcock, which I didn't shoot at because I couldn't get the safety off in time.

Dull stuff for anyone but me. But in the long-from-now perhaps some family member who didn't know me can get a sense of who I was from reading those scribbled pages, and I will live again, if only in the perceptions of another.

Some time back, *Gun Dog* magazine offered an attractive hunter's diary with replaceable inserts. The cover was leatherette, the insert nicely conceived with space to enter the date of the hunt, area hunted, weather conditions, companions, dogs used, guns used, points, flushes, retrieves, and details on the bag, as well as a page for comments.

Few bought them, and the magazine quit offering them. Perhaps they were too pricey. After all, you can make a fine journal of a Big Chief notebook from Kmart. Some use account ledgers, which are hardbound, durable, and cheap. Marginal diarists, I suspect, are more inclined to be faithful to something they paid dearly for than to a schoolkid's lined tablet.

A diary or log should be small enough to fit in your gear bag or box so it's always handy. The point of a diary is to record your day while it's still immediate, not several days later, when you come home.

I have a "possibles" bag, a stout canvas carryall about the size of a big purse, with several compartments. In it I carry shooting glasses, some dog medications and salves, a roll of elastic bandage in case I sprain something, gun-cleaning equipment, extra batteries for locator collars, and my diary. I fasten a ball-point pen to the page where the next hunt will be recorded.

From December 1, 1984: "Breakfast huevos rancheros," I wrote. "They were great. Ted presented me with a compass that belonged to 'dat's me and my kar,' Eric Gustav Heinrich Miller."

Ted Lundrigan is a lawyer hunting buddy from Minnesota who had handled the estate of an old fellow and had inherited some small items none of the survivors wanted, including some photos of the old man back in the 1920s. One, showing Eric Gustav beside a flivver, had scrawled on the back, "dat's me and my kar." I'd laughed about it.

The small brass compass is old and unspectacular, but it generated an idea for a short story with supernatural overtones that later appeared in *Sports Afield*.

In the "comments" section, I wrote, "Got into an endless field of standing corn and cockleburrs way over our heads. Worst mess I ever saw. Spent half-hour at car picking burrs and listening to Willie Nelson."

I remember that field of cockleburrs. I later wrote an article titled "The Great Burrfield Massacre."

I killed only one quail but bagged two pieces of writing. Most trips aren't that productive.

Some days are less sunny: "Horrible day. Got parking ticket at office. Stupid goddam bureaucrats. Magazine won't pay for trip. Paid too much for a videotape. Nothing in the mail. Everything wrong. So, Ginger busts the only covey we saw—my steady dog. I jumped two scatters in a milo field and missed a hasty, but wide-open shot."

There are two entries, separated by nearly ten years, that I would give anything not to have written. One was January 10, 1985: "Today is the day I lost my hunting buddy. Foster died last night. There's no space here to record thirty-seven years of memories."

And on September 11, 1993: "Guff died today. My old friend of twelve years died last night at the vet's. Doc said something toxic. Marty and I buried him in my shell vest near the old log across the lake. Put one of my walking sticks as a marker and his collar around it with a couple of shotgun shells.

"I loved that old dog and will never forget him."

There is more, but it makes me sad to recall these memories. They are not the entries I return to when the hours are small and my legs are weary. I'd rather read about the days of sunshine and birds. Yet those dark moments are part of the fabric of a hunting life, and it would not be right to exclude them from the skein of events.

I've filled nearly seven of the gunning-diary inserts, and if I'm lucky I'll fill many more before I unload my gun for the last time.

# 10

# FEEDING THE INNER MAN AND DOG

ALL GOD'S CHILLUNS got to eat. Especially the hunter and his dog, who by midday have burned enough calories to heat a hockey rink.

There are three meals in a hunter's day—or most everyone else's, for that matter. It begins conventionally enough with breakfast. I used to think that all breakfast cafes featured hard, tasteless little sausages, greasy eggs, and soggy toast, but the Cenex truck stop at the Mitchell, South Dakota, exit off Interstate 90 left me stunned, not to mention stuffed. A platter, not a plate, of biscuits and gravy—thick with tasty chunks of sausage, creamy and not gelid, the biscuits light and flavorful. The tab was $2.99. Of course, it really isn't in quail country.

Most cafes feature hockey-puck biscuits and coffee sufficiently corrosive to delaminate tank armor. There's always a tableful of local experts where you can hear a rundown on farming, foreign affairs, and last night's television.

The evening meal—supper in the real world of mid-America, dinner in more refined places where no one owns bird dogs—usually is eaten, as we say in Missouri, "back to the house." The hunt is ended and we're showered, shaved, and wearing trousers that won't turn briars and aren't decorated with bird blood. We eat good home cooking in a civilized setting.

The only true hunter's meal is lunch.

The midday meal is the bridge between the halves of a hunt, and without a good one the hunter is risking a midafternon slump.

I know a man who dove hunts with gentility. He brings a hamper with cheeses and perhaps a bottle of wine. If there are animal guts stuffed with meat, it's not the common hunter's fare (weenies or supermarket summer sausage) but exotic sausages from the deli, delicate in taste and digestive effect.

But Chuck is an aberration. More often I've hunted with guys who scrape the congealed grease off the top of a can of Vienna sausages, stuff a couple of them between crackers that were stale when Black Jack Pershing was a second lieutenant, top the whole awful mess off with a bilious swig of Nehi Orange, and call it lunch.

I like to eat well. I was born to be a ne'er-do-well playboy, except someone forgot to furnish me with the money to fund my exotic tastes. Champagne taste and a Grapette budget. That means I usually wind up eating hunting lunches that would have to improve to qualify as garbage.

I don't know why, other than that I am easily led, but for several years I used to lunch at a grocery store in a little town in north Missouri that should have been defunct years ago (both the grocery and the town). The store's major concern was selling Big Smith overalls, cotton work gloves, and thin rubber boots for slopping hogs, but there was also what for want of a better term I'll call a deli counter.

It was as close to a real delicatessen as *Hee Haw* is to *Die Walküre*. Typically, what they called "cooking lunch" involved a white-bread-and-rat-cheese sandwich and a foaming Big Orange plopped on the scarred and dirty counter.

If you were in a mood for hot food you could order a hamburger and fries. The burger shined with stale grease and smelled like the bottom of a garbage can. The fries were limp with soaked-up oil and encrusted with layers of salt. Terrible food. You deserve better, after three or four hours slogging through briar patches and swamps in quest of quail.

The same goes for the dog, who has earned a good meal more than you have. He has covered five or six times more territory and done it at a much brisker clip. He probably has at least one painful bruise and a few cuts from fence barbs, stobs, and briars.

He won't complain if you throw some dry dog food on the ground, may not even realize he's being shortchanged, but are you willing to risk confronting St. Peter, who may be wearing a shell vest and a frown? "So you're the guy who fed your dog lousy food, eh?"

Before the hunt I offer dry dog food tricked up with a splash of vegetable oil (butter-flavored gets their attention). They think they're getting something special and will eat the oiled food when they won't touch dry food.

I carry a few packages of the "burger" type foods (Gaines-burgers, for example) for a midmorning snack or lunch. Even though it may not be as nutritious as good-quality dry dog food, it's tasty, and the dogs gobble it as though it were ground round.

Some dogs don't hunt flat-out and don't burn as many calories. They'll stay in trim all season, but hyperactive setters and pointers turn to skeletons no matter how much or how often you feed them.

Some hunters don't feed the dog until the day is over. They believe "a hungry dog hunts better." Dogs need fuel just as we do. You try going without breakfast and see how long you last.

I AM PARTIAL to mom-and-pop cafes. Moms have a reputation for putting good, simple fare and plenty of it on the table, and pops have a reputation for insisting that mom fix good chow. If I walk into Ethel's or Ruth's and an ample woman with a bosom that looks as if she's smuggling soccer balls says, "Y'all just have a seat over there and I'll be by as soon as I get the turkey out of the oven," I know I've stumbled into the Mom lode.

John's is such a place. A mile up the road from where Jesse and Frank James robbed the Katy Railroad, John's has early Formica decor, and the floor has angles that have long abandoned plumb and level, perhaps aided by an unreported earthquake or two. John's has its own intrinsic charm. The clock on the wall not only tells time but also has a motorized rotary drum with little placards that drop to reveal advertisements for hog feed and funeral parlors. You can raise pigs or die at John's and be taken care of.

The place violates William Least Heat Moon's dictum. Moon, the author of *Blue Highways*, said that the more calendars on the wall of byway cafes, the better the food. There are none at John's, because time really doesn't exist and nobody cares what day it is anyway. In Otterville, today is just like yesterday, and tomorrow won't be any different.

It was in Ottervile that I, bleary from an insufficiency of sleep and coffee, spied a sign, partially obscured, that read: ". . . tique." I always stop in backroads antique shops, figuring someday I'll find a Parker Invincible being sold for twenty-five dollars by a little old lady who is afraid of guns and just wants to be rid of the thing.

The proprietress was sweeping off the sidewalk, and I walked up and said, "Mind if I go in and look around?" She stared at me as if I had just asked to see her underwear and clutched the broom to her, obviously wishing it were a .357 magnum. I shrugged (no telling what quirks distress Ottervillians) and walked in—to a beauty parlor. "Boutique," not "antique." I slunk out past the alarmed beautician and fled.

John's has a lunch special that will lie in your stomach until supper like a comfortable brick. You have a choice of three side dishes to go with Italian steak and great scoops of mashed potatoes with real homemade gravy. And then there's the obligatory chunk of home-brewed Dutch apple pie.

Outside in the car the dogs are busy fogging up the windows and perhaps eating somebody's birds if the game bags aren't secured. You did do that, didn't you?

Ah, John's—as far up the gastronomic spectrum as the little north Missouri cafe is down. I still wonder if that place had dirt floors. I was afraid too look too closely.

I ate in another north Missouri joint that I was *sure* had dirt floors, until the barmaid's baby crawled across it and mopped a clear spot with a wet diaper.

For every dozen of those hellholes, there is a gem, a gleam among the dross.

Three of us, stubbly and gritty-eyed, stumbled into a central Missouri restaurant one noontime and had a sumptuous meal, cooked by Moms—three of them, and they fussed over the meal as if it were a family reunion.

At the end of the entrée (a word that would have meant absolutely nothing to anyone in the cafe) we were asked if we wanted pie. The key word, amid "apple, cherry, and lemon meringue" was "gooseberry." Now, for the disadvantaged, gooseberry pie is as close to Heaven as anyone ever gets on this earth, and infinitely closer than any bird hunter ever will. The green berries, their tartness defused by sugar, make pie filling second to none, and if the slice of still-warm pie is topped with good vanilla ice cream, Nirvana is at hand.

We all ordered gooseberry pie.

The grandmotherly waitress reported in distress, "There's only one piece of gooseberry pie left."

We all looked at one another, discarding multiple murders in favor of flipping coins for the pie. I won.

"But we're your guests," they whined. I looked at them with compassion.

"Screw you," I said. "I won and I'm going to eat the whole damn thing."

I did and it was wonderful.

Once, three of us headed home after a grueling hunt and, hungry as tenement rats, stumbled into a Friday happy hour at a ramshackle old hotel. The bar looked like a *Gunsmoke* set, but there was a sideboard groaning with barbecued chicken wings and various good-for-you things like cauliflower, broccoli, and mushrooms, all of which you could dip in an array of concoctions designed to make you want more beer.

We bought a beer each for a half-buck, and proceeded to eat twenty-seven dollars' worth of free food. I understand the free food's still available, but a sign at the door reads "No service to anyone without shoes or shirt—or wearing brush pants!"

Spence Turner once brought a bottle of ten-year–old red Cabernet to a camp-out in a kitchenette-equipped motel. The wine perfectly complemented a meal of filet mignon, baked potatoes, and tossed salad.

I thought I had risen to a greater glory after that meal, but one of the dogs threw up in the middle of the night and Spence, rising to recycle the wine, stepped in it.

A WELL-KNOWN outdoor cooking writer once wrote about how to take care of quail, and I disagree with just about everything the writer said.

For example, "field dress as soon as possible." I've carried shot quail all day for as long as I've hunted and rarely field dress them until after the hunt, unless the weather is unusually hot or the bird is badly shot. I've noticed neither off-taste nor spoilage.

If you're finicky, gut the bird immediately. I've tried knives with gut hooks and never could get them to work, so I separate the bird between the breastbone and spine enough to fish out the guts with my fingers.

"Never risk ruining your birds with freezer burn. Wrap each quail tightly with a piece of heavy duty plastic wrap."

I freeze quail in zip-close plastic bags with enough water to cover them. I honestly don't know how long this extends freezer life, but we've run across forgotten packages a year later and the birds tasted just fine.

Guy de la Valdene, whose book *For a Handful of Feathers* (Atlantic Monthly Press, 1995) is as good as quail writing gets, says, "I view skinning birds with the same critical eye I reserve for those who cook their meals inside plastic pouches—a desolate habit of those who can only be described as the premature ejaculators of the culinary nineties."

Well, that pretty well sums it up.

But I can skin a quail in a tenth the time plucking takes. We usually fix quail in a casserole, where they don't dry out. If all you do with a quail is panfry it, plucking would help.

Here's how I prepare a quail for the table:

You'll need a good pair of poultry shears. Cut off the wings and feet, and pull off the head. Split the breast skin with your fingers and work the hide over the wing stubs and neck, down the back and over the legs, twisting off at the tail. Pick off loose feathers. Insert the shears along the backbone at the neck, cut down the spine and angle at the pelvis, following the pelvic girdle. Repeat on the other side of the spine. You can strip out the guts and backbone with your thumb. Use your thumbnail to pull away the rib cage on either side. The quail is now clean inside. I usually remove the legs from the breast for cooking.

Guy, as his name would imply, is a first-rate French chef, and his book offers many exquisite recipes for quail and quail fixins. Once I ran into another French chef and collected his quail recipe, sort of.

Chef Stephane bought an old fraternal lodge building in Niagara Falls, New York, and planned to turn it into a fine French restaurant. I hope he did, for this was several years ago and I don't know if it survives.

When Tom Huggler discovered the place, it had one semideveloped floor and two floors of neglect. But Stephane—I have no idea what his last name was—radiated enthusiasm and optimism. He *would* generate affection for French cuisine in Niagara Falls, where the main topic is snow. Sometimes in July.

We brought our own wine and sat around a Salvation Army table on sofas and chairs rescued from yard sales. Chef Stephane obviously was operating on a low budget. But his meal was the stuff of dreams. A clear consommé was followed by several courses that flowed like the seasons. And we finished the night with Kay Ellerhoff singing the love aria from *La Bohème* to the good chef, who was discombobulated. Before we left, I asked him if he had a good recipe for quail, and I jotted down incomplete notes (wine and food dulled my reportorial skills). This is what he said:

## STEPHANE'S QUAIL

Slice onions, oranges, and potatoes into a Pyrex or stainless-steel casserole dish to make a bed on which the quail will lie.

Baste with a juice of spices and herbs (not specified) and Grand Marnier liqueur.

Roast at 300 to 350 degrees, with a water-filled bowl in the oven to provide moisture. Don't overcook.

(I don't quite understand this part:) Boil raisins and squeeze and add to cream, with herbs, and simmer till thick. Add mushrooms and chives or scallions at the end of the cooking. This sauce, I think, goes over the quail before serving. A friend guesses you add boiling water to the raisins and let them steep for 10 minutes to refresh them, squeezing out excess moisture so they'll absorb the cream.

For the side dish, serve potatoes sautéed with onions and garlic.

I am not a good cook, but I think anyone with kitchen skills can take my garbled report and turn out a wonderful dish.

SYLVIA BASHLINE wrote the finest wild game cookbook ever: *The Bounty of the Earth Cookbook* (Lyons & Burford, 1994). You can order it from Lyons & Burford or by calling her: 814-632-8568. Here's a good recipe from the book—a grouse recipe adapted to quail:

## SYLVIA'S QUAIL

Dress quail as described above, removing the backbone (save it for stock). Separate breasts and legs. Figure two quail per person and we'll consider this a recipe for four.

In a heavy iron skillet, heat two tablespoons of cooking oil, two of butter or margarine. Dredge quail pieces in flour, salt, and pepper to taste, and brown in the skillet. Place the breasts on the bottom of an ovenproof casserole dish, the legs on top of the breasts.

In a bowl mix a cup of chopped mushrooms, a cup of a good dry red wine (I use Cabernet Sauvignon), a cup of plain yogurt (Sylvia uses light cream), and a pinch of tarragon.

Bring this to a boil in the skillet and pour over the quail; bake covered for an hour at 350 degrees. It may take less than an hour for quail, which are smaller than grouse.

If there's enough liquid left, use it as a sauce over wild or brown rice; if not, pour all of it over the quail and enjoy. I think a Riesling is a fine wine to accompany this wonderful dish.

It's a toss-up between Sylvia Bashline and my wife, Marty, on quail cookery. Sylvia has the edge on salmon and other creatures that we don't encounter often, but give Marty a Missouri quail and she is Superwoman of the Kitchen.

## MARTY'S QUAIL

Brown six quail in butter or oleo. Brown about two cups of chopped fresh mushrooms in the drippings and transfer to a baking dish. Drain a can of artichoke hearts and brown in the drippings, adding more butter or oleo if necessary. Transfer to the baking dish.

To the same browning pan add one cup of chicken broth and one cup of white wine; cook to blend. Pour over the browned birds in the baking dish. Cook in a low oven, about 250 degrees, for one hour or until the birds are done. Serve with wild rice or noodles.

HERE ARE THREE more quail recipes whose origins are lost in the murk of my filing system.

## QUAIL FLAMBÉ

Ingredients: Ten quail, cleaned and skinned; salt and pepper; $^3/_4$ cup butter or margarine; 1 teaspoon dry basil; $^1/_2$ cup plus 3 tablespoons brandy; $4^1/_2$-ounce can of black olives, chopped.

Directions: Sprinkle quail with salt and pepper. Melt butter or margarine in a large frying pan over low heat. Stir in basil. Add the quail and sauté for 7 minutes. Add $^1/_2$ cup brandy and olives and stir. Cover, reduce heat, and simmer for 25 minutes, basting often. If more liquid is needed add more brandy.

To flame, bring quail to the table in the pan. Uncover and add 3 tablespoons brandy; light with a long taper.

## QUAIL WITH ARTICHOKE HEARTS

Ingredients: Six quail, split down the back; salt; 6 table-spoons butter or margarine; paprika; 1 can (16 ounces) artichoke hearts, drained; ½ pound fresh, whole mush-rooms; 2 tablespoons flour; ⅔ cup chicken stock; 4 table-spoons cream sherry.

Directions: Sprinkle birds with salt. Melt 4 tablespoons of butter in a large skillet. Place quail skin side down in the skillet and brown on both sides. Put the quail in a deep casserole and sprinkle with paprika. Place artichokes between quail. Add 2 more tablespoons of butter to the skillet and sauté the whole mushrooms. Add the flour to the mushrooms, stir, and gradually add the chicken stock. Cook for 4 minutes and add the cream sherry. Salt and pepper the gravy to taste, then pour it over quail. Bake covered for one hour at 350 degrees.

## PARMESAN QUAIL

Ingredients: Eight quail split in half; 1½ cups cornflakes, crumbled; 1 teaspoon celery salt; ¼ cup Parmesan cheese; salt and pepper; 1 teaspoon sesame seeds; 1 cup evapo-rated milk; 4 tablespoons margarine or butter.

Directions: Mix cornflakes, celery salt, Parmesan cheese, salt, pepper, and sesame seeds. Put the evaporated milk in a bowl and dip the quail in the milk, making sure both sides get wet. Roll the quail in the cornflake mix and place in medium-hot saucepan with butter or margarine. Sauté until done—about 25 to 35 minutes.

IT WOULDN'T HURT to pour a little (very little) gravy or sauce over some dry dog food for the faithful animal companion that helped you put the meal on the table.

It'll probably upset his digestion, but he'll thank you for it.

# 11

## MY FOUR-FOOTED PARDS

RECENTLY, MY WIFE was cleaning out the dog pen while I was sky-larking around the country enjoying myself. She took along a cordless phone in case someone called to offer cheap manure removal (or perhaps a contract hit on an absent husband).

As she pirouetted around piles of dog poop, the phone slipped from her pocket, described a one-and-a-half gainer in midair, and plunged mouthpiece first into a steaming pile of former dog food.

Somehow that brief but memorable moment sums up much of our life. But for each of the disagreeable moments, there have been many of joy, of companionship and contentment.

While Marty possibly wouldn't agree, at least with my enthusiasm, dogs have been a major part of life for us for many years.

I couldn't be without them, and I suspect, despite a phone that smells faintly like a kennel, neither could she.

The movie *American Graffiti* involves a fleeting moment when a blonde in a Thunderbird cruises past one of the principal characters and mouths the words "I love you." He spends the rest of the movie frantically trying to find her.

If nothing else, it proves that extended ideas can result from pinpricks of time when feelings crystallize. I had such an epiphany once. I was driving through the country when a motion in a yard along the gravel road caught my eye. It was a puppy in the act of sitting. My vision was blocked for a moment, then I cleared the obstacle and saw the whole tableau.

This puppy was no prize. He was a lovable, vaguely Labradorian type, but white with brown spots. If anything he looked a bit like Nipper, the Victor Talking Machine dog who cocked his head at His Master's Voice.

A small boy, perhaps seven or eight years old, stood in front of the puppy, his hand outstretched, his manner authoritarian. The puppy vibrated, his energy barely contained by the command.

In that fleeting instant a lifetime leapt into memory. The lifetime was mine. These two eager youngsters were setting out together on one of life's great adventures, that special relationship between someone and a dog.

The puppy faced his first master. Not only did the dog belong to the youngster, but the boy had been charged with its training.

At that age dog training is a mutual adventure, for the boy will learn as much from the dog as the dog will from the boy, and in the learning, they will learn trust and a deep love that only death will sever.

A lump came into my throat, for I knew that death would intrude on this sweet picture, and I could only hope that the dog would live beyond its biological norm and the boy, grown to near manhood, still would love the grizzled and stiff old mutt that his puppy would become.

HIS MASTER'S VOICE, a special voice to any dog. My dog then was Guff, a French Brittany who was both hunting partner and good friend. I tend to be overly sentimental about my dogs, an emotional drawback when it comes to that bruising moment when they die.

But on the other hand, my joy in them must be enormously more gratifying than that of the person to whom a dog is a trained creature, marginally more personable than a barn-lot cow.

Guff slept in a doghouse in a kennel, but in his mind he was always a human who deserved mashed potatoes, gravy, stew, and whatever else the big folks were having.

He was my friend and confidant, and though he may not have understood the words that described the specific trouble, he understood my moods perfectly, and there was no one more unfailingly sympathetic or more attentive (unless, of course, someone scraped a plate elsewhere in the house).

Chaps was my first dog, a cross between a springer and a cocker spaniel. She came as a pup when I was ten years old, and when she died I was married and the father of a child.

She really wasn't my dog, though. I didn't train her; she actually owed her allegiance to my father, for whom she energetically hunted squirrels for many years. It was his delight to head into the ten acres of woods in what we called The Bend (an elbow of the Chariton River) with the cocky little dog and a single-shot Winchester .22.

Chaps taught me how to dog play, though—how to get down on dog level and have a tremendously good time wrestling and tumbling. I still do it, unseemly behavior in a man closing in on the doddering years, but I enjoy it as much as I did when I was ten years old.

Nothing is more fun than rolling around with puppies, getting the front-room rug all balled up, filling the house with shouts, barking, and dog hair.

If ever I get up from one of those silly sessions feeling foolish, I might as well jump off a cliff, for I have become "mature," which in my book is the same thing as becoming useless. Dogs, used right, can keep you young.

Bird dogs drag you over endless hills and through brush patches where Brer Rabbit would have recoiled in horror. All that exercise is perceived to be good for you. At the end of a long day in the field, legs rubbery, knees twinging and creaking, breath ragged, and throat raw from dust and yelling at errant mutts, I find the therapeutic values of hunting and hiking are arguable. But chances are, the lean old hill hunter will live a bit longer than he would had he just camped in front of the box watching glandularly disturbed youths try to rip one another's heads off on Saturday afternoon.

And if his heart quits somewhere beyond the ridge you can see from the house, don't worry about his soul. You may find the body, but the spirit is still bounding toward the distant fencerow, which looks *so* good.

MY DOG FRIENDS are in the kennel now, watching the house. Someone always is on guard for the slightest flicker of movement that might mean a door will open. And when a door opens, a person might emerge dressed in brush pants and carrying a gun. And that *does* mean someone is going hunting.

Paroxysms of anticipation, unrestrained barking, unreasoning joy. This goes on during all daylight hours and sometimes at night. I suppose I could electrify the barkers and cow them into silence, but let them have their hyperkinetic happiness. Their lives are short.

Pepper is aging, her once black face now a patchwork of gray and black. She is Guff's daughter, and if Guff were alive he would be sixteen years old. I suspect that he still would insist on hunting. But he lies on the far hill by an old log, and I still visit the grave and swallow at the lump in my throat.

Pepper's eyes have the opacity of age. But she still jumps wildly at the gate if I leave the house, still wants to play keep away or dog tag or any of the silly games that old men and old dogs remember.

By coincidence, I'm listening to Frank Sinatra, another old entity who has aged well. And the song he is singing, by ironic coincidence, is "Young at Heart."

Pepper's two oldest children, Dacques and Chubby, are my mainstays, with a decade of experience behind them. Dacques was the firstborn of Pepper's nearly thirty youngsters. He is built like a running back, compact and hard as a brick, tight-muscled, with the gait of a rocking horse.

On a recent five-day hunt, the other dogs, all younger, were limping and footsore after the first couple of long, hard days. Dacques? He bounded out of the kennel every morning, without a trace of stiffness, and asked only how long it was until he got to hunt again.

Chubby is softer, longer haired, and appealing. He was a leftover puppy, not chosen by anyone, because they wanted females or a different color or had some other reason.

Marty and I came home from the airport, where we'd shipped his last two siblings. I looked at the little puppy in the kennel so alone, wondering where his family went, and told Marty that no power on earth would make me sell that puppy. It was a happy decision. Chubby has been my confidant, my friend, my sleep toy for ten years.

He's no longer chubby. Midway through hunting season I can feel his ribs, though he still looks stocky. He was the fat one in the litter, first fastened to Pepper's mainline faucet, then sprawled in the middle of the puppy-chow dish, ever expanding his canine beltline.

He was cute and cuddly and lovable. He wriggled all over with the delight of being alive and of being my dog. He also was the first of the litter to hold a game bird in his mouth, trotting uncertainly here and there with worried eyes, flustered by the stirrings of his birthright. And he released the dove with reluctant jaws, but had not chewed it or gotten it all spit-draggled.

Now he is my dead-bird expert, rarely losing one. He retrieves to hand and I get a dry bird, not one slobbered. He will go into the water after a bird he can see, and he loves to swim. He has become King of the Bluegills, swimming in endless figure eights after the fish he knows are there but can't see, except from the dock above.

Chubby's intelligence gleams from his eyes. When you look into the eyes of some dogs you know nobody's home. Chubby is always there. He listens, he understands, he empathizes. "He knows everything I say," I tell Marty, and she just shakes her head.

DOGS ARE A mixed blessing. You can't guarantee getting a wonderful companion any more than you can guarantee getting a beautiful child, as joyous as conception might be.

Ginger was a tribulation, but she demonstrated the axiom that if you wait long enough things generally turn out okay. She was a Brittany without papers. She belonged to a friend of a friend, a young couple with two small children.

She was wild-eyed and wild, so full of energy, a bowling ball to the kids' pin. They spent more time in midair than they did on the ground. She wasn't mean, just supercharged.

And that's the way she hunted for two years. She made big-running pointers look like they were backpedaling. She left the kennel like a drag racer, and no amount of shouting would keep her in sight.

It's just that she was of the elements, motivated by primal drives and forces from far out in the Universe. She heard commands that I didn't give. She lived to hunt, and no love is greater than that, including the one she had for me.

Where the average dog is content polishing his master's shoes with the underside of his muzzle, the Out There is what Ginger wanted. There were horizons yet untouched by the lean bitch who troubled my life for nearly a decade.

Ginger was part cat, I think. Inscrutable. I never knew what was behind those nutty eyes, those amber orbs that glowed and shone with an alien life.

But one rainy day on a trail in northern Minnesota she put it together, me and the birds and her, an equation that she had been unable to solve. Maybe it was the miserable weather, maybe it was experience and maturity, but suddenly she was working in front of me, side to side, and pointing grouse. That was the turning point.

There were lapses, but they were few. She grew old and then she got sick and died at the vet's, an apparent heart attack. My old girlfriend was gone and the emotions she'd raised in me over the years no longer were tangled. All the frustration and anger and confusion vanished, replaced by love and sorrow.

I REMEMBER Ginger and Chip and Guff, the ones who are gone, and I still feel pangs of sorrow. I still miss them, especially Guff, who was the best dog friend I ever had.

Guff was all things—silly and playful, sweet and understanding, serious and businesslike. He knew what was called for in any situation. He was not the best bird dog I've had, but he was totally adaptable. He made up for a lack of nose with an abundance of desire and brains. He was my dog and I was his man. It was a workable arrangement.

Guff was not above misdeeds, and some were awesome in their destructiveness. As I sweated copiously to build a house for him (he already had reduced a sleeping-bag pad to filler for a high-jump pit and the goose-down bag that went with it to something that looked like a massacre at a poultry ranch), I draped a brand-new, expensive hunting jacket on the gatepost.

I forgot it. Guff climbed atop his new house, stretched out, and seized the sleeve in those iron jaws. When I reclaimed the jacket it was a rag that would have been scorned in a hobo jungle.

Marty always wanted a pool table, no matter the reason. A game of eight ball was a vision she held in her mental hope chest, one that, being married to an always penurious outdoor writer, she was not likely to realize.

But she came into a bit of money, and instead of buying a spare barrel of oatmeal for our puling bairns, she went downtown, clutching her entitlement, and shortly was followed home by a pool table.

About that time I got Guff, then an eleven-week-old French Brittany with big brown eyes and soft fur like that on a cuddle-doll. He was my baby. He snuggled in my lap, looking up at me with eyes that promised unvarying fealty.

Ah, he could do no wrong!

Guff ate the pool table. I don't mean he ingested the entire thing, just its crucial parts: the corners of the pockets, so that shooting in a ball was like driving a Volkswagen into an airplane hanger. It takes some of the skill out of the game when you can use a fencepost as a cue and shoot beach balls into the pockets with room to spare.

Merely getting atop the table was a climbing feat equivalent to Tenzing and Hillary scaling Everest. There was no way a pup his size could have climbed there—but he did, just as he learned to climb out of a six-foot chain-link-fence kennel like a capuchin monkey.

Considering the intense use to which a Brittany puts his chop-pers, it's no wonder he needs regular dental care. My local pet-supply pusher said, "You *must* take care of your dog's teeth!"

What I should have done was pull them, not take care of them, but instead I arrived home with a tool, apparently cast of twenty-four-karat gold judging from its cost, that looked like something for checkering gunstocks.

"This will remove that *terrible* tartar from your cherished dog-gie's teeth!" the guy exclaimed, looking like the actor on televi-sion who dresses in a white lab jacket and holds up a toothbrush and a tube of goo and implies that if you don't use the goo, your jaw will fall off.

Have you ever tried chiseling plaque off the flashing teeth of a writhing Brittany? It's marginally easier than giving a vasectomy to a bobcat.

It does no good to bellow, "*It's for your own good!*" in the dog's ear, for bird dogs understand only "Let's eat!," "Biirrrd!," and, "I'm gonna knock your thick head off!"

It was that last suggestion that moved Guff to sullen acquiescence, though I found later that evening that he'd peed on my thousand-dollar stereo speaker. You can talk all you want about territorial marking and biological imperatives; that dog was getting even.

Once, Guff lodged a shard of something he'd gnawed—possibly a suit of armor or a Sherman tank—between his gum and tooth and swelled up until he looked like a cantaloupe with ears.

I told him it was a visitation from God, but talking theology to Brittanies is a waste of time. They only want to know when they're going hunting.

Guff was short for McGuffin, which is what Alfred Hitchcock called the gimmick in all his movies that both the good guys and the bad guys sought. The McGuffin is what everyone wants.

Guff was a quail dog first and foremost. Since he saw grouse only once a year, he tended to forget they aren't just big quail who'll sit right under a French Brit's black nose as if skewered there with a dirk.

Grouse are stupid birds, brainless and indecisive. Anything foreign in their environment throws them into a mindless confusion that usually leads to movement—they either walk off or fly up in a tree, where they can be taken in what one of our hunters euphemistically refers to as "the preflight position."

A French Brittany creeping forward like a roan cat definitely qualifies as "foreign," and Guff had trouble realizing that he should instantly freeze at the merest whiff of grouse stink, no matter the direction; that he should not try to locate that smell or make it grow stronger.

One day lingers in my memory, not because it was so good but because it was so bad. Guff started it by falling off his bed. He'd sneaked up onto the overstuffed chair in the old cabin where we stayed and, probably dreaming of cute little freckled ladies, rolled over and onto the floor with a thump that woke everyone up.

Later, Ted Lundrigan and I walked the edge of a doghair-popple stand that crowded a pasture. I searched the thick saplings in vain for the noble sight of my dog, descendant of champions, as he coursed the covert. Then a movement caught my eye in the field beyond.

There was my noble dog snacking on a cow pie, his shoulder drooped and twitching like Charles Laughton in *The Hunchback of Notre Dame,* ready to roll in what he didn't eat. It may come as a shock to new dog owners to think that their endearing companions will eagerly snack on bovine biscuits, but life with bird dogs is filled with such taut moments of unhappy discovery.

My Zen calm went out the window, and I roared ancient Anglo-Saxon while Ted tried to pretend he was hunting alone.

I lost it again after the third point Guff busted. My resolve to practice Zen calm went the way of my resolve never to touch Scotch and water again, never to buy another shotgun, never to lie about my shooting.

I laid unexorcisable curses on Guff. I held him by the cheeks while I explained in dog language what I expected. Dog language is sheer, roaring filth that even the most inane creature comprehends.

Perhaps Guff pointed a grouse that day, but if so it was done while I wasn't with him. I do know that he busted at least a half dozen birds, most of which had been nailed by Ted's setter, Salty, until Guff came along like a derailed cattle car.

You can steal a man's children, corrupt his wife, ruin his business, even insult his baseball team—but let your bird dog bust up a point that his bird dog has made and you've really ticked him off.

Ted began to look at Guff as if he were head lice, then looked at me as if I were the head. Salty was becoming jittery, Ted was becoming . . . well, homicidal is the word that springs to mind. Fortunately, the sun took pity on me and started to go down. We headed back to Pine River. Guff, of course, had to assist with the driving, his face between us, panting a fog of recycled manure.

Back in the cabin I regaled a bored audience with tales of Guff's misbehavior. "He was disgraceful," I said. "He made every mistake in the book and invented some new ones. He was terrible." As I spoke, Dave Mackey's face grew alarmed, and I thought it was with horrified sympathy. It wasn't.

"Watch out!" Mackey exclaimed. "He's sick!"

Guff threw up on the carpet behind me, a slurry of awfulness that took an hour to clean up. Guff looked at me with sick apology, and suddenly I felt sorry for the little guy and tried to consider the big picture. After all, for every bad day he'd given me so many good ones. For every point he'd busted he'd made a dozen good ones in the past.

So I petted the little dog and he sighed heavily and pouted off to a corner to lie atop Dave Mackey's hunting pants, which were draped over his box of ammo and gun-cleaning gear.

Dave picked up his pants the next morning and they were dripping with WD-40. Guff had lain on the nozzle of the full spray can and emptied it.

THESE ARE THE memories I dwell on, now that Guff is gone and no amount of sorrow will bring him back. We had fun—my God, we had fun. He was a dozen years of sunshine in my life and only a few moments of shadow.

That's what the dog/hunter partnership is supposed to be. When I count my blessings, and they are many, that partnership is prominent.

# 12

## SHARING LIFE AND THE FIELD

**THEY'RE GRAYING,** gimpy, and grizzled, and as familiar as your hunting britches or the suspenders that hold them up.

They groan a lot in the mornings, but they go all day.

Hunting buddies. Like good wine or smelly cheese, they age well.

Back in 1954 BRC (Before Ray Charles), pop singer Kitty Kallen sang "Little Things Mean a Lot." The song is hokey and dated, but it could be the anthem of bird hunters on how to treat hunting buddies.

It's not the big things you do for each other, it's the little things.

There should be a bumper sticker: "If you ain't got hunting buddies, you ain't got . . . "; well, never mind the rest of it.

No bird hunter is complete without someone to share the rips and tears. If you endure cold and sleet and come in tired and beat with the world in shreds around your shoulders, who can you really share it with except your hunting buddies who were there with you? No one else understands. Or cares.

A few bird hunters are solitary, rarely going afield with others. They must either have psychological strength or lack of it. It isn't natural to hunt alone all the time.

Everybody enjoys the occasional lone hunt, like a rogue wolf on the prowl. When you hunt alone you owe allegiance to no one, need follow no one else's direction. It's just you and the dogs.

But that's not the same as sharing a good hunt with a friend. If you spend too much time alone you'll congeal, scum on a pond. People need cross-pollination, like good plant stock, to thrive and grow.

I've been blessed with good hunting buddies—and cursed with one bad one.

Andy, my youngest son, is among the good ones. He's been hanging around with me since he was five. He's twenty-five now, with his own double and bird dogs.

He went with me to a duck camp, scarcely out of toddlerhood. The overheated old farmhouse sweated with outrageous stories and deliciously nasty language, and I could see Andy's little synapses sparking and knew that he was storing information like a CD-ROM. That he still hangs around with me, knowing what he does about my flaws and faults, is the measure of his friendship.

You check hunting buddies out carefully, like used cars. They may have hidden faults—rust underneath or clanks in the transmission. It takes a lot of driving to judge mules, used cars, and hunting buddies.

I made one mistake. Some years back I courted a guy I

thought would be a wonderful addition to my hunting buddies. He was charming, funny, intelligent, knew bird hunting, talked a tough game.

He was a sham.

He threw away friends like Handi Wipes. Once three of us were quail hunting. My Brittany, Chip, went on point just as I happened over the hill. Mr. X was behind the point (he *did* have a facility for finding the action), and he didn't see me at the top of the hill.

It's accepted that if a dog is on point, you holler "Point!" and wait for your buddies to share in the action. Mr. X carefully looked around, didn't see me watching him, decided he had the point all to himself (with my dog), and flushed the birds.

I showed myself and asked how come he hadn't let us know the dog was pointing. "Oh, I was going to," he said. "But the dog bumped the birds and I had to shoot."

On another hunt, Andy was a green kid with a new gun, out with the big guys for the first time. It was late afternoon and he hadn't shot; he'd been out of position on every flush. Now he was off to one side as my dog, Chip, pointed in front of my erstwhile friend.

"Hang on," I said. "Let Andy get a shot." Andy trotted down the hill to the dog. Mr. X was just behind Chip, and he very deliberately stepped forward, flushed the covey, and shot.

"The dog was going to bump them," he said, though the dog hadn't moved.

Andy and I walked out of the field and went home. Today, many years later, Andy hunts with me, and Mr. X has moved on to shed a couple of wives and a few more people who considered him a friend.

People like him forget to pay their share of hunting-trip expenses. I thought it was carelessness or absentmindedness, except it kept happening.

Somehow I always busted the brush while he walked the perimeter and picked off easy shots. I'd do the dishes, and he'd be funny and charming to guests while I was elbow-deep in soap-suds and gritting my teeth.

Finally it sank in that he took advantage of everyone. He didn't forget—he just figured friends were disposable, to be used up and discarded.

He was a textbook example of how not to treat your hunting buddies.

I've developed a set of commandments. I didn't go to a mountaintop to get them, engraved on stone; I just walked a thousand miles over brush country, swamps, and prairies.

This is what you do:

1. Buy your buddy's lunch sometime for no good reason.

2. Remember his birthday and get him a scurrilous card that will make him laugh. Present it in front of your mutual friends. I'm saving one for Spence Turner that reads, "When I get as old as you, I hope like hell I smell a lot better."

3. Praise his dogs.

4. If you double on a bird, it's his—and you say, "Nice shot!"

5. If you travel together, you pay 50 percent of the mutual costs—and it wouldn't hurt to volunteer a little extra. Buy a round in a cowboy bar and say, "You get the next one," even if there is no next one.

6. If you promise something, bankrupt yourself, sell your kids, whatever you have to do to make sure you fulfill the promise.

7. Ask his advice on things. He probably is smarter than you anyway.

8. Laugh at his stories and jokes, especially the ones you've heard five times before.

9. Don't talk about him behind his back. We all have faults, and you are not God's chosen messenger to point them out.

10. If he screws up, forgive him. If he hurts your feelings, let him know—chances are he didn't realize it and will feel awful. Grudges are postcards from Hell.

THESE ARE TEN commandments only because ten is a well-known number when it comes to commandments; there are many more. It boils down to this: Accept your hunting partners like your mate—for better or worse.

Phonies like Mr. X are not creatures of human fault and failing; they are mean and self-centered and they should be no one's hunting buddy. They are the true lone wolves.

Spence Turner has been my hunting buddy for about twenty-five years. We met in a training seminar and found that my mother was from a town in Wisconsin only a few miles from where he grew up.

But we found a more lasting bond than that—we both live to hunt game birds. Spence is an English setter man, and I guess he can be forgiven for that. We all have a dark side. I, of course, believe that the Brittany, more specifically the *French* Brittany, is God's own bird dog.

Spence is worth a book. He refers to himself as "a rotund trout biologist." He's not just any trout biologist—he's the best in the country. Missouri has a limited trout fishery, especially in streams, but Spence has managed, in his career, to maximize its potential and to create a trophy mentality that keeps the fishing outstanding.

That's tough duty among Ozarkers, to whom any fish is just two fillets awaiting their dusting of cornmeal and flour.

For all his professional grace, Spence has an uncanny penchant for self-mutilation in his personal life. Once, in an effort to trim off some weight, he took up jogging.

Each morning, he would rise at 5:30 and lumber down the road in the dark—until he fell off the side of the road, ripped up his ankle, and was out of commission for quite a while.

Another time he tried his hand at car repair and managed to drop his ancient Volvo station wagon on his thumb. Only because his wife, Joan, pulled into the driveway as it happened was Spence saved from spending the day like a coyote with its paw in a leghold trap.

Spence's Volvo is worth another book. If the Swedish company wants endorsement, Spence is the man. This vehicle has been driven about the same number of miles as the starship *Enterprise*, only it doesn't look nearly as good. Spence now drives a new Ford pickup, but somewhere the Volvo is still clattering down the highway, faithfully eating miles, no doubt harboring dark secrets in the detritus under the seats.

Spence, as far as I could tell, never once cleaned the vehicle in all the years he owned it. There were old pop cans, Styrofoam coffee cups, fishing lures, crumpled maps, half-eaten sandwiches, broken sunglasses, and a hundred indefinable objects that crunched or squished underfoot.

I once rode to and from Wyoming with Spence when he had a serious sinus drip, and the level of used Kleenex rose about to the dashboard, like a snowdrift in a blizzard.

There's still a pocketknife of mine somewhere in the vehicle, but we never could find it. It's probably just another blob of rust by now, indistinguishable from the rest of the car.

The brace that kept the rear hatch door from falling on your head quit working early in the life of the car, so Spence carried a stick to prop up the door. Getting something out of the back end became a flirtation with the guillotine. You never knew when the thing would fall.

The top of Spence's PortaPet kennel got squashed in somehow. It would have taken thirty seconds to pop it back to full height, but Spence doesn't work that way. The seasons rolled along and his leggy setters crouched in the compressed kennel, peering out like trolls under a bridge. The kennel door, of course, wouldn't snap shut, but Spence solved that problem by positioning the kennel so that when the Volvo hatch was shut, the kennel gate couldn't be opened. Or so he thought.

Spence's stopgap solutions are like an invitation to the Devil's ball—you may be honored at first, but you know there's danger in the future. Once Spence was supposed to work in northeast Missouri. He left the morning before, with a full complement of bird dogs in portable kennels, his clean clothing in a duffel bag on the passenger seat beside him (unzipped, of course). Spence intended to hunt the afternoon before working, check into a motel, clean up, and go to work the next morning.

He also had a bag of snacks handy. He almost always does. This time it was chocolate-covered raisins, about two pounds of them. Spence considered this health food. Raisins are good for you, he reasoned; we won't talk about the chocolate.

Spence left one bird dog in the PortaPet, with the Volvo hatch down against the kennel gate. As any hunting-dog owner should know, it is folly to leave a bird dog alone anywhere except, perhaps, in a maximum-security cell with attentive armed guards. The confined dog, knowing its kennelmates and master are having fun without it, is a loose cannon, a bomb with a sputtering fuse.

Spence's setter somehow managed to scoot the kennel backward until it could force the gate open enough to squeeze out. The dog then oozed up over the top of the kennel, shredded one of the seats, and, not content with that, ate all the chocolate-covered raisins. Now let your imagination dwell on the effect of two pounds of chocolate-covered raisins on a dog's digestive system. The dog proceeded to vent both its frustration and its intestines on Spence's open duffel bag.

Spence trudged back to the car after a couple hours of quail hunting, saw the wreckage of his car and clothing and, exhibiting his priorities, howled, *"He ate my raisins!"*

MY FIRST LONG-TERM friend was Foster Sadler. Our friendship began forty years before we buried him. Spence and I sat side by side in the little country church where a minister tried to sum up Foster Sadler. I don't know what Spence was thinking about, but I suspect his thoughts were close to mine. He too had spent countless hours in the old farmhouse on the hill and in the fields of the Mussel Fork.

We were an unlikely trio of musketeers: writer, biologist, and teacher. But we fit. We enjoyed one another, and we each had our reservations about the pointless homilies of the churchman.

That minister never had been quail hunting with Foster, therefore he really couldn't have known him. It was his loss, but our loss was far greater.

Foster was the big man on the Keytesville campus. Our Keytesville High School graduating class totaled twenty-three.

Foster was a running, gunning left-handed forward on a basketball team that went 21–3, the best in Keytesville history. He also was a hard-throwing baseball pitcher.

He was lanky and threw what we called a drop, what they now call a sharp curve. I was his catcher because I was the only player on the team who didn't have enough sense to get out of the way of those devastating curves, which dove into the dirt and often bounced up under the chest protector. I had bruises all through high school from blocking those wicked drops, but we won when he pitched.

When we weren't playing ball we hunted quail together, sometimes behind Coach Sadler's bird dog, a marginal pointer named Joe, sometimes by ourselves. It was inefficient, but we saw a lot of country.

After high school we went our separate ways for a while, but I never found a friend I liked any better, and when I moved back to Missouri as a young married breadwinner, Foster and I resumed quail hunting together, just as we had in high school.

We walked an incredible number of miles over the Green Hills of north-central Missouri. We started no later than 9 A.M. and usually went until it was too dark to see. Often we'd get back to the old farmhouse in total darkness.

We cooked and survived belly-busting, high-cholesterol meals. Stinking wet dogs slept here and there, and feathers from long-dead game birds eddied in the sharp winds that shook the old house in the gut of winter. I often slept on a lumpy, narrow couch whose only virtue was that it was next to the stove. I was uncomfortable, but warm.

Foster had roamed these hills for years and knew them intimately. The Green Hills actually are higher in elevation than the vaunted Ozarks, but the rolling topography isn't as dramatic: just pastures and woodlots and bottom crop fields.

All the little north Missouri towns were dying, victims of better transportation and roads, chain stores and discount prices. But we'd stop at some crossroads gas station–cafe–grocery store and eat terrible lunches that rumbled in our guts all afternoon. It was the price you paid for dozen-covey-a-day hunts.

Foster was an outdoorsman in the true sense. He would rather be outdoors than in, and he didn't mind being by himself there. He was pleased to have company, but the lack of it didn't bother him. He read books by naturalists for pleasure but already knew most of what he read through personal experience in the woods and fields.

Outdoor professionals were impressed by his knowledge and liked him because of his personality. Foster could walk into a bar and within minutes would be deep in conversation with a stranger, usually someone who started talking to him because he looked— what, sympathetic? Likable? Something. People respected him.

One summed it up after he died. "He was one of the good ones." It should be on his marker.

Foster was six foot two, most of it legs. He had the stamina of a deep-chested pointer and was as hard to keep up with. On some of those lowering evenings on the Mussel Fork, far from the car, my muscles grabbed so painfully that I went to my knees with tears in my eyes. But I went on because Foster did and I didn't want to be a quitter.

We never talked much about problems unless they were universal and concerned the outdoors. We'd cuss dams and habitat loss, but not personal unrest. The shared time was our refuge from troubles, and by unspoken agreement, we didn't bring up life's frets.

We shot quail and hunted turkeys and deer. We camped in snow and rain. We fished and canoed and walked the lovely hills with heavy backpacks. We watched prairie chickens boom in the spring and once saw a hawk chase a small bird in deadly aerial ballet.

Foster would call and suggest a canoe trip. The first one I ever took was with him. The Current River was high and muddy and it looked like the north Missouri catfish rivers we'd grown up by. But Foster knew of a spring branch; we hiked it and I could see the bottom and little fish swimming as if in the air. I'd never seen clear water before. "That's the way it's supposed to be," he said.

It seemed there could be no end to our times together. We hunted pheasants together in Iowa and went another time to the far end of Kansas, where Foster killed a prairie chicken. We hunted together in South Dakota and hiked the little creek where Custer found gold and precipitated the Sioux war that ultimately did him in.

Where didn't we go? We went to northern Iowa for a Czech festival at Decorah, floated the Upper Iowa River and ate lefse. Once we floated almost all the Brule River in Wisconsin. We were on the river for almost a week and caught only one fish, a trout scarcely big enough for walleye bait.

Once we backpacked into a Missouri wilderness area and camped on an old logging road. We woke in the middle of the night with the tiny tent illuminated as if by alien visitors, and we realized after sorting out our confusion that some deer jacklighter in a four-wheel-drive had nearly run us over.

Foster got a Brittany who slumbered in his lap while he watched television. One day he let her out of the kennel to run and she was hit by a car. He didn't say much, but I knew he hurt. Today I have six Brittanies, and every so often I hug them close and wonder if I'm worrying about them or grieving for my friend.

After Foster got through teaching me about much of the upper world, he took me caving and introduced me to the world underground. He got me into bicycling and downhill skiing. We hunted turkey in his family's woods overlooking the Mussel Fork, and I shot my first turkey there.

There were Indian burial mounds on that ridge, and I wonder if it wouldn't have been more appropriate, even if a bit bizarre by society's standards, to have buried him there. The Indians knew where the sun set and where the day's warmth began.

Once we camped along a creek in Texas County (naturally, Missouri's biggest), and beavers slapped the water in the night, a sound like stones being dropped off the bluff into the water. I nearly stepped on a copperhead, and Foster nearly shot a turkey. The nearlys were as good as the successes. I always learned something.

Foster knew conservation better than I did, though it was my business. He knew the land and how it worked, and he spoke the language of the creatures who lived there. He hunted, but he also bird-watched. He took long trips just to see sandhill cranes migrating.

There's an old joke about a bird-watcher, asked by a rustic type what he's doing, who says, "Well, we want to watch birds." The rube spits in the dust and says, "Watch 'em what?"

Foster knew there was no "what." You watch wild things because you have a kinship with them and because their lives are uncomplicated, elemental, and easier to understand than the complex and murky lives of people. Foster should have been born a great hawk, adrift on angry winds, hunting for his life but also glorying in the fierce joy of flight.

Once we went to Wisconsin to ski and I caught the flu. On the way home, Foster and his wife stuffed me in the back end of their tiny pickup truck, swaddled in a half dozen sleeping bags. A woman slid into the truck at a stop sign, denting the bumper slightly. She was distraught and peered into the back, where I lay in misery, and said, "I hope your son is all right!"

Foster was only six months older than I, but maybe he was my surrogate father. He always took the lead, and I always let him. In most groups I tend to jump in front and shoot off my mouth, but around Foster I never did. I was comfortable with being a follower. He knew where we were going and why we were there, and I didn't question his judgment.

Foster mattered in a world where leaders are morons and imbeciles rule the roost. He never hurt anyone and he never made war. World leaders parade center stage with a fistful of bombs and the understanding of maladjusted children, and we all suffer the threat of life's end.

Foster and I met at the Lamine Wildlife Area for what turned out to be our final hunt together. It was November 21, 1984. My hunting diary says, "Perfect quail hunting day. Sunny and in the 40s."

Typically, Foster had first discovered this nearly six-thousand-acre area, though it's closer to where I live than to where he did.

We used my dogs; Foster was without a bird dog by then. It was, as I look at it in retrospect, a winding down. He had dogs when I didn't, and then I had an ever-increasing number of bird dogs and he had none.

We hunted along a creek bank, put up a covey, and Foster shot a bird. I missed mine. We looked a long time at a ford and finally decided to chance it. There was a scary moment at midstream when the truck spun and seemed to bog, then it lurched free and came out the other side.

This was new country, only glimpsed from the usual hunting area. I looked at the area map and found we could have come in from the west, but not without a long roundabout.

We hunted a nice-looking outholding of the area with no luck. "Let's see if we can find that chunk," Foster said, indicating another scatter from the main body of the area. We jounced down a thinly graveled road and around a bend to a low-water crossing.

The stream was beautiful, clear water running over the concrete slab and spilling into a deep, crystalline pool. Downstream there were gravel bars and riffles. It looked like a smallmouth haven. "We gotta go fishing here!" I said. "This is beautiful!"

Foster agreed, and I said, "As soon as it gets warm I'll give you a call, and we'll give it a shot."

Foster died on January 10.

I temper with no qualification the affection I felt for Foster. Wherever I go in the outdoors the rest of my life, he will be there—for he was there. He beat me to the mountains, the streams, the prairie. Then he came back to take me along to share in his enthusiasms.

Everything I am in the outdoors, I owe to Foster Sadler. My father put a gun in my hands, but after he was sidelined by ill health Foster was my constant hunting companion. I can't comprehend that we will never again hike the hills or camp by the side of babbling waters.

You can't reduce a man's life to a pitiful few paragraphs and insufficient locutions. You ought to dim the stars and let the moon pay homage. It has taken a decade for me to write about Foster. The pain has ebbed, and the good memories remain. I'd like to think that there is more of Foster than memories, that he's in the winds and the woods and the waters.

If there is reincarnation, Foster could be a morel mushroom popping up from the rich loam of the Mussel Fork bottom, where he always spotted the shy fungi much more readily than I did and always had a fuller tote sack. Or he could be a buzzard circling the Mussel Fork bottom on the uplifts of a sunny spring morning, or a buck deer ghosting through the dawn mist.

But I hope Foster comes back as a big tom turkey who trumpets his virile challenge to a spring dawn when life is erupting from every pore of the earth. I hope he lures in some dumb hunter and makes a fool of him and sends that guy home with a sheepish grin, saying, "Boy, that ol' turkey was smarter than me!"

I still sit on the ridgetop and watch the sun come up and feel the peace that dawn gives me. But who will meet me at the camp to share the retelling?

SEVERAL YEARS after Foster died, I was driving home from a Minnesota grouse hunt. I took the back roads through north Missouri, and they gradually became more familiar as I neared the Mussel Fork country.

And then I was on the road that leads past the church where we buried him. I pulled in and stopped. There was no traffic; there seldom is on this winding, forgotten county highway. It was late afternoon in mid-October. Leaves from the old trees in the churchyard lay tired and tattered on the graves. The sun was bright, but the air was chilly. Quail season would begin in two weeks.

I looked at the marker for a while, trying to think of something appropriate, not mushy or inadequate. There was nothing to say. Henry Thoreau wrote, "The sad memory of departed friends is soon encrusted over with sublime and pleasing thoughts, as their monuments are overgrown with moss. Nature doth kindly heal every wound."

The marker still looked new, not weathered or moss-covered. I set a couple of shotgun shells upright on its base. Grass grew on what I'd last seen as raw earth. Life moved on.

Across the road and a few yards closer to home was an open field that Foster had bought to plant Christmas trees. The trees were big enough for sale, but no one had tended them.

We'd hunted the field and always put up quail.

I stood by the car, reluctant to leave, but with no reason to stay other than memories. A quail whistled sharply over in the field. It was almost time to covey up for the night, and I headed home.

# A FINAL WORD

QUAIL ARE A declining species. I'm not implying that they will become endangered, not in my lifetime or that of my children.

But quail habitat has shrunken dramatically in the past thirty years, and there is no relief in sight. Programs like the Conservation Reserve are temporary panaceas. They don't really cure anything—they just delay the decline.

The root cause? Too damn many people and too much technology. Short of the Apocalypse, we're not likely to change either. People continue to breed as if the world were infinite, and we're still trying to gouge maximum profit from the land with little regard for its other inhabitants.

Agribusiness and the economy dictate larger farms run by fewer people. In a business there is no room for quail or for idle hours spent in sport. More people move from the few remaining family farms, take jobs in the city, and, within a generation or two, lose their ties to the land.

City families often are single-parent, and that parent works. Who teaches a kid to hunt quail? It's difficult not to be pessimistic, given the realities of the way it is compared with the way it was.

Quail hunters owe it to their sport to join a conservation group and fight whatever delaying battles are possible.

Quail Unlimited was founded in 1981 and has a membership of about 50,000. That's fewer than the number of quail hunters in my home state of Missouri. Obviously, many quail hunters *don't* belong.

Contact QU at Box 10041, Augusta, GA 30903 (803-637-5731). Included in membership is a subscription to the association magazine.

I've long felt that the Izaak Walton League, although not specific to quail, is the most closely attuned to what I do. There are 54,000 members—again, a small group, but a strong voice nationally.

The league is an effective lobby group, lean and mean. It doesn't spend big bucks on administration, as do some of the larger conservation groups.

Contact the Ikes at 1401 Wilson Blvd., Level B, Arlington, VA 22209 (703-528-1818). Membership also includes their magazine.

Also worthwhile is Pheasants Forever, Box 75473, St. Paul, MN 55175 (612-481-7142). It is the largest of the three, at 72,000 members. The group led the fight to preserve the Conservation Reserve Program (which benefited pheasants more than it did quail). There is also a magazine included with membership.

These groups must be supported. They are our voice in national politics, where the individual has little voice. Complain to your representative and you'll get a pat on the head from an aide.

Unless you're a very rich quail hunter, you can't even come up with a congressional-level bribe. You're bucking big economic interests. The only hope we have is a group effort that gets attention.

You must remember that Washington is a world unto itself and that, once entangled in that political web, even the best-intentioned politicians forget their roots.

Conservation-oriented people go to Washington and become old pols. I've seen it happen to people I know and once respected. It isn't pleasant, and the consequences for those of us who remain on and of the land are depressing. Our champions cave in.

But they do recognize pressure. They are susceptible to being leaned on.

So lean.

Hard.